CHARLIE'S FAMILY

CREDITS

Charlie's Family
An Illustrated Screenplay
Written by:
Jim VanBebber
ISBN 1 871592 94 1
CREATION CINEMA COLLECTION, VOLUME 10
© Jim VanBebber 1998
All world rights reserved
"Manson Movies" © Jim Morton 1998
"Death Valley And Beyond" © Jack Sargeant 1998
First published 1998 by:
CREATION BOOKS
Design/layout/typesetting:
PCP International

Author's acknowledgements
Special thanks to: Kathy Franks, Ed Lang, Phil Anselmo, Kevin Crompton, Ross Karpelman, Dwayne Goettel, Sherri Rickman, Jim Klein, Julia Reichert, Karim Hussain, Mitch Davis.

"YOU KILLED ME FIRST" copyright © 1985, R. Kern; used with permission of Richard Kern.

CONTENTS

Introduction by Jack Sargeant   V

CHARLIE'S FAMILY   9

Appendix One: **Charlie's Family: Selected Storyboards**   151

Appendix Two: **Manson Movies** by Jim Morton   164

Bibliography   185

Index Of Films   187

INTRODUCTION
DEATH VALLEY AND BEYOND

I first saw Jim VanBebber's **Charlie's Family** on its unofficial American premier, at the Chicago Underground Film Festival, in the summer of 1997. The film was not even an official festival entry, but was screened as a 'work in progress', as Jim explained shortly before the midnight screening: the film needed a little more post-production work, a few wipes and fades, to make it match his vision.

Jim VanBebber has been working on **Charlie's Family** for much of the last ten years, the film growing organically, from its original inception as a docu-drama, to its ultimate incarnation as possibly the final word on the events of August 1969, and beyond. Juxtaposing incredibly detailed recreations of key historical events against interviews with Family members, and a group of current Manson-obsessed, nihilistic, teen killers. The entire narrative itself is woven, tighter than a midnight creepy-crawl, around an imaginary true-crime television documentary on the Family and the slayings. The lengthy time frame in which the film was produced worked well for VanBebber, the cast aging enough over the shooting schedule to portray both the youthful death-obsessed hippies, and their later – contemporary – incarnations as convicted killers.

VanBebber's technical prowess, unique vision, and the sheer depth of his research, means that the film manages to resonate with the audience's media-directed collective experience of the events, via the careful manipulation of familiar images and iconography. So, for example, at various points throughout the movie VanBebber opens or closes a sequence with a shot derived from contemporaneous news footage of the trial, or based on scenes from Lawrence Merrick's excellent, and rarely seen, Spahn ranch commune documentary **Manson** (1972). At other points, VanBebber utilizes various in-camera film manipulations to create horrifically perverse scenes of twitching violence, the visceral nature of which is punctuated by the manipulation of the shooting speed of the film.

It was Richard Kern who first introduced me to VanBebber's movies. I remember sitting in Kern's East Village apartment, in the dark, watching VanBebber's deeply disturbing short **Roadkill: The Last Days Of John Martin** (1988). The film – a trailer cum short – depicts, in a lucid detail rarely seen in cinema, one man's descent into nightmarish cannibalism and complete madness. At the film's climax John Martin, who has already been depicted eating road-kill, dismembers a luckless driver while his half-naked girl friend looks on, from a cage built on top of a stove. As John Martin finishes his grisly task he turns to face the woman and ignites on the stove beneath her. Cut to black as she screams.

As the film ended I remember turning to Kern, who was laughing at both the film's grim climax and my evident shock. "Pretty cool, huh?" he stated. I knew I had to find out more.

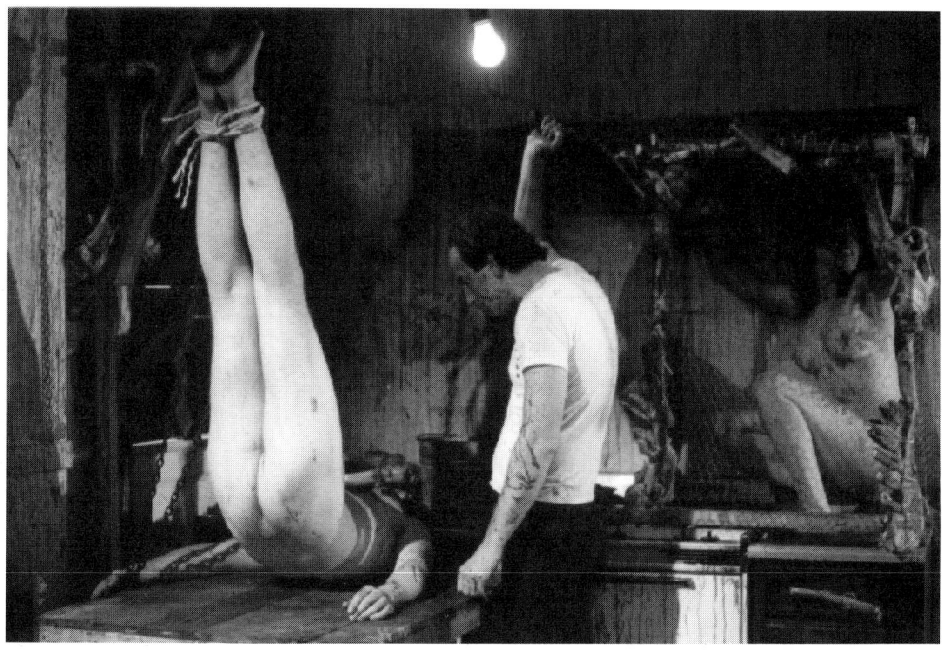

Roadkill: The Last Days Of John Martin

VanBebber is a native of Dayton, Ohio. A natural born filmmaker, he began producing Regular 8mm movies as a teenager, once using his talent for persuasion to get all of his friends, family, and neighbours to act as zombies. In 1983, VanBebber won a scholarship to Wright State University's Motion Picture Program on the back of a forty-minute film, **Into The Black**, described as a Kung-Fu Rock-Opera. At Wright State he studied 16mm film production under auspices of the documentary filmmakers James Klein and Julia Reichert, both of whom had been nominated for an Oscar in 1983, for their film **Seeing Red**. At the university VanBebber also hooked up with his producer and Director of Photography Mike King, as well as various future members of his cast who were studying dramatic arts at the college.

VanBebber never graduated, instead – realizing that he was familiar enough with 16mm – he used his third year college loan to purchase ten rolls of film, and started working on the feature film **Deadbeat At Dawn** (1987), a movie that took three and a half years to complete. Part homage to biker pictures of the sixties such as Corman's **The Wild Angels** (1966), Anthony Lanza's **The Glory Stompers** (1967), Lee Madden's **Hell's Angels '69** (1969) and Richard Rush's **Hell's Angels On Wheels** (1967), **Deadbeat At Dawn** starred VanBebber himself as reformed gang-leader Goose, out for vengeance following the brutal murder of his girlfriend. While lacking the developed stylistic innovation that VanBebber utilizes in **Charlie's Family, Deadbeat At Dawn** makes up for it with its sheer relentless velocity. Shooting hit-and-run-style, without permits, and on a low budget, VanBebber managed not only to act in and direct the movie, he also edited, designed and coordinated the special effects, having taught himself the basics after studying

Deadbeat At Dawn

Tom Savini's work in George Romero's **Dawn Of The Dead** (1979). He also performed his own stunts, including several highly choreographed fight sequences, crashing a car into a river, and – most dramatic of all – jumping from a high dam into the shallow waters below. Not content with just pushing himself to the limits, VanBebber also pushed his cast. While shooting pick-up shots to enhance the film's climactic fight sequence, one of the cast – Tom Burns – broke his thumb. VanBebber required three more takes following the accident before he was satisfied that he had captured the required footage. Such was the dedication of the actor that he did not even protest.

Following **Deadbeat At Dawn**, VanBebber produced the fifteen-minute **Roadkill: The Last Days Of John Martin**, building the set in his basement, and personally collecting roadkill from the highway in order to dress the set. While a short film in its own right, **Roadkill** was also a trailer for a potentially longer project, designed in part to raise funds for a feature. Three years later VanBebber repeated the exercise, working from a script by horror aficionado, and editor of *Deep Red* (1990) and *Horror Holocaust* (1996), amongst others, Chas Balun. VanBebber directed the short/fund-raiser **Chunkblower** (1990), with the aim of using the footage to raise money from potential investors. Unfortunately, the project never amounted to anything.

VanBebber directed another short in 1983: **My Sweet Satan**, loosely based on the true story of Long Island Satan Teen Killer, Ricky Kasso. The film follows a group of lower-middle class Death Metal fans as they drop acid, fuck, and, eventually, kill. Once again, VanBebber played the lead and, in one notable sequence, was required to hang himself. Ever the dedicated

My Sweet Satan

filmmaker, VanBebber obliged and – due to the unsatisfactory harness he was wearing – nearly killed himself in the process. The scene – of course – looks great. The film was an underground success and, following its screening at the First New York Underground Film Festival in 1993, was named Grand Prize Winner.

And then there was **Charlie's Family**. Constantly in the background, always edging forward in piecemeal fashion, as finances dictated. An epic project which Jim would allude to in interviews over the years, offering tantalizingly brief glimpses. Ten years in the making, as Jim VanBebber and Mike King hustled money to complete the film, and VanBebber honed his vision down to the visceral mind-fuck that the finished film promises to be, defying the odds to bring the brutal, relentless vision of the slayings to the world.

As Manson's visage vanished from the screen, and the lights came on, the Chicago audience began to applaud. Jim received a standing ovation. As did the cast, who had flown in specially, many of whom have had nothing to do with the film since principal shooting ended four years previously. Jim is currently – at the time of this writing – completing the editing.

He is obsessional, driven, and visionary.

This book offers a taste of the mayhem to come.

—Jack Sargeant, Spring 1998

CHARLIE'S FAMILY

An Original Screenplay by:
Jim VanBebber.
A cinematic meditation inspired by true events and court transcripts with fictional elements.
Copyright © 1992 Mercury Films, Inc., all rights reserved.
Written and Directed by:
Jim VanBebber.
Produced and Photographed by:
Mike King.
Editing by:
Jim VanBebber and Michael Capone.
Costume Design and Wardrobe:
Sherri Rickman.
Make-up and Special Effects:
Jim VanBebber and Andy Copp.
Associate Producer:
Michael Capone.
Production Manager:
John Mays.
Music by:
Charles Manson, Phil Anselmo, Ross Karpelman, Download, Down, Body and Blood, and Superjoint Ritual.
Additional Music by:
Jimmy Rodgers, Kenny Richardson, Ernie Nisley, Evangeline Noel, Kevin Engle, Marty Romie, Dale Hughes, Tim Arnold and Don Neibert.
Production Crew:
John Bradley, Tom Maher, Rob Creager, Mark Shuster, Steve Bognar, Greg Doddson, Marco Fargnoli, Josh Winteringham, Thanos Foutouras, Shaun Baker, Tom Burns, Jeff Barklage, Nate Pennington, Joel Pohlman, Richard King, Bill Yoe, Rob Wagner, Thanos Fatouras.

CAST

Charlie	Marcelo Games	Barbra	Meirika Girten
Tex	Marc Pitman	Lil' Patty	Alydra Kelly
Patty	Leslie Orr	Katie	Samantha
Sadie	Maureen Allisse	Mojo	Ernie Nisley
Leslie	Amy Yates	Jennifer	Stacy Valencia
Bobby	Jim VanBebber	Danny	Rob Zinser
Clem	Tom Burns	Kenneth	Tim Hedges
Linda	Michelle Briggs	Brooks	Tony Brown
Snake	Sherri Rickman	Bo	Lisa Feathers
Rose	Mariposa	Paul	Andy Copp
Dennis	Steve Riley	Zezozoze	Jimmy Yoe
Catherine	Ann Howard	Pooh Bear	Elliot Quinn
Country Sue	Megan Mateer	Tanya	Courtney Macy
Stephanie	Kym Olsen	Joe	Jim Lockard
Ouisch	Cathy Carver	Al	Brian McKay
Brenda	Kris Hall	Biker	Scott Thatcher
Mary	Annette Reckart	Lotsapoppa	Don Keaton
Sunshine	John Gnann	Gary	Kevan Curren
Kaye	Jennifer Orr	Young Man	John Lockwood
Susan	Mary Blacklock	Large Man	Charlie Goetz
Juan	Mike Bazzini	Short Man	Sam Turcotte
Terry	Mark Gillespie	Dark Haired Woman	D'aun Edmunds
Jerry	Paul Harper	Blonde Woman	Tina Martin
Old George	Norris Hellwig	Husband	Geoff Burkman
Randy	Joel Pohlman	Wife	Sharise Parviz Berk
Simi Sherri	Valerie Hatt	Shorty	Nate Pennington
Biker	Mike Zengel	Ronald	M.M. Jones
Bloody Mama	H.M. Kelly	Jack Wilson	Carl Day
Rosina	Cecelia Horstman	Bob	Jim Sayer
Shorty's Wife	Denise West	BBC Host Ian	Gary Thompson
Sleeping Woman	Kim Pennington	Reporter	Dan Crawford
Clarence	James McCullars	Police Officer	Henry Pant
Biker	Alan Joyce	Police Officer	Candy Johnson
Dennis	Jimmy Hearse	Police Officer	Tim Montgomery
Mars	Freddist	Police Officer	Linda Struve
Stevie	Josh Hoke	Voice of Satan	Phil Anselmo
Lucy	Andrea Layne		
Darren	Darrin Brown		
El Padrino	Michael Krieger		
Corpse	Jennifer Rickets		
Satan	John Bognar		
Old Charlie	Dill Bowling		
Todd	Tom Ramey		
Stan	Tony Wilson		
Gypsy	Melissa Schlosser		
Squeaky	Marita Clarke		
Sandy	Kellye Morris		
Nancy	Sara Quoia		
Kitty	Kim Hall		
Cappy	Mel Clark		

FADE UP FROM BLACK

[Title Card: "1969"]

> A fast-paced montage of horrific images follow, voiced over by Patty's speech which joins the final shot.

[IMAGE: LINDA, LESLIE, Beatles poster, gun, finger on trigger, gun barrel, LOTSAPOPPA, SHORTY, BOBBY, HUSBAND tortured by PATTY and Leslie, CHARLIE, fire, skull, TEX stabbing, Tex as Satan, the DARK HAIRED WOMAN, the BLONDE WOMAN, SATAN laughs. Shadow of a hand with a knife, knife in the Husband's neck, SADIE laughs, the LARGE MAN; beaten, Patty laughs, knife dripping blood, the Blonde Woman choked on Noose, Leslie laughs, the Blonde Woman screams, Patty in the rain, in black and white]

PATTY: You better wise up, the time is gonna come when all men will judge themselves before God. It'll be the worst Hell, the worst Hell on Earth. It'll make Nazi Germany look like a picnic. And you gotta be ready for that, right now, right here, right now, just like that! And that's where we're at all the time...

[IMAGE: Tex in courthouse hall with Media, Leslie, in courthouse hall with Media, bald X-heads on corner of Temple and Broadway, SANDY press conference, SNAKE with mirror, Patty with Husband holding mirror, which reads "Rise"]

GYPSY (V.O.): If somebody needs to be killed, there's no wrong, you do it and move on.

SANDY (V.O.): There's a revolution coming very soon!

[EXT. DAY – Street corner of Temple & Broadway.]

> A group of Charlie's supporters sit vigil outside of the Hall of Justice.

KENNETH: You've lit the fuse yourself. We're gonna cut and chop all you fuckers up.

[INT. DAY – Crowded press conference.]

Stevie (right).

Sandy sits, calm amongst the cameras, lights and microphones.

SANDY: L.A. will burn to the ground. Los Angeles will burn to the ground. Once again, you've judged a reflection of yourselves.

GYPSY (V.O.): We are what you have made us.

[FADE UP FROM BLACK]

[Title Card: "1996"]

[INT. NIGHT – Bedroom inside the house of MARS]

> It is a surreal scene. Inside of Mars' Bedroom, a very spooky place, are gathered MARS, LUCY, DENNIS, STEVIE and EL PADRINO. Stevie is tied to the single bed, his legs shackled to a spreader bar with a live microphone jammed in his mouth, secured with clear tape. Mars stands above him, periodically zapping him with an electric cattle prod. She is wearing a metal talon glove and a red, white and blue strap-on dildo, on her face. Across the room, Lucy, a skinny young girl, is cutting words from magazines, preparing a letter, ransom note style. Next to her is El Padrino, a skinny, distressed looking kid in a cape. He is conducting a demonic invocation with gun powder

Lucy.

and a scepter. Watching over all of this is Dennis, skinny and tattooed, confident. He is applying make-up to his face to resemble a skull. These young, white kids are heroin and crack dealers.

The screams of Stevie are filtered through the recordings of the Rev. Jim Jones, whom the group listens to for comfort and strength.

REV. JIM JONES (V.O.): Children, hurry. No way I'm gonna do it. I refuse. I don't know who fired the shot, I don't know who killed the Congressman, but as far as I'm concerned, I killed him. You understand what I'm saying? I killed him. He had no business coming, I told him not to come. Die with respect, die with a degree of dignity. Lay down your life with dignity, don't lay down with tears and agony. It's nothing but death, it's just like Max said, it's just stepping over to another plane. Don't, don't be this way. Stop these hysterics... this is not the way for people who are Socialist/Communist to die... no way for us to die. We must die with some dignity. We must die with some dignity. Then they'll have no choice, we have some choice, now we have some choice, oh God. It's never been done before, you say... it's been done by every tribe in history, every tribe facing annihilation. All the Indians of the Amazon are doing it right now. They refuse to bring any babies into the world, they kill every child that comes into the world. Because they don't want to live in this kind of world. Be patient, be patient. Death is... I tell you, I don't care how many screams you hear, I don't care how many anguished cries. ...Death is a million times more preferable to ten more days of this life. If you knew what was ahead of you, if you knew what was ahead of you, you'd be glad to be stepping over tonight. Death, death, death is common...

> Suddenly the attention in the room is drawn to a small television set. On the screen is JACK WILSON, a tabloid news journalist, promoting an upcoming special episode of his series, "Jack Wilson's Crime Scene". He greets the viewer from a Courtroom set.

JACK: One week from tonight, join me, Jack Wilson, for a special edition of Crime Scene. We're gonna journey back to August 9th and 10th, 1969.

> The image on the screen shows Snake in black and white.

SNAKE: We're waiting for our father to be set free.

JACK: Two nights of murder that sent terror through Los Angeles and ultimately, the world.

> The screen shows black and white footage of the bald-headed followers, outside the Hall of Justice.

X HEADS: Judgment day is coming, people!

JACK: Next week on "Crime Scene", we're going to bring you face to face with the evil few, who forever poisoned the Love Generation, as I talk with the members of Charlie's Family. Hear the jailhouse confessions of Leslie, the Homecoming Queen, twisted by Charlie into a knife wielding maniac. Bobby, the unknown linchpin of the Family, who committed the first murder. Sadie, now a Born Again Christian, once Charlie's most outrageous disciple. Patty, a former Sunday School teacher, she found Jesus Christ in Charlie, and Tex, the former High School football captain, who became Charlie's bloodiest butcher. In Charlie, they found a Daddy, a Lover, and a Savior. And it only took his words to ignite within them a rampage of hate and murder.

> Mars unstraps the American Flag dildo from her face and stares at the television. Dennis has completed his make-up and is wearing a top hat and a cape. He looks like a White Baron Samedi.

JACK: The actual killers, bringing into focus, for the first time, their years as members of Charlie's Family.

[DISSOLVE]

[Boiling, red blood. Superimpose over title: "CHARLIE'S FAMILY"]

[INT. DAY – Jack Wilson's video post-production suite]

> The camera pulls back from one of the many monitors within the editing and dubbing consoles. Jack's editor, BOB, works on the footage. On the monitor is Leslie, now age 47.

LESLIE (on screen): Oh, we did so many drugs, and it made sense, and we were sure that it would work.

> Jack Wilson enters the suite, carrying the mail. He sits down opposite Bob, who is eating a cheeseburger.

BOB: How's your day going, Jack?

JACK: She's back up for parole at the end of this year...

[INT. NIGHT – Prison C.I.W.]

LESLIE: My parole hearings are taped and broadcast...

[INT. DAY – Jack Wilson's VPP Suite]

> Jack looks away from the video monitor.

JACK: I'm glad it's not up to me... She seemed very sincere... but so did Susan... I will say that I think Leslie will be the next member of the Family to be paroled.

> Jack picks up a package, wrapped in plain brown paper, from the mail in his lap.

JACK: No return address on this one...

> Jack rips the brown paper away, revealing a shoebox. He opens it and pulls out a letter and VHS tape.

BOB: What the Hell is that?

> Jack reads the letter. It is composed of cut out letters from newspapers and magazines glued onto a red piece of construction paper.

JACK (reading aloud): "To the pig producer of the movie on Charlie..."

Jack Wilson opens his mail.

>Jack hands Bob the tape.

JACK: Hook up the half-inch machine... I want to see what the Hell this is...

BOB: Okay...

[STRAIGHT CUT]

>The television monitor behind Bob's head shows color bars. Bob fast forwards the tape. Suddenly, on the screen is a black and white videotaped medium shot of Charlie in his jail cell, facing the camera. Charlie gyrates strangely.

CHARLIE (on screen): The powers of the serpent, that live inside all that is true on the line of Infinity... Infinity... speaks through all life... in the voice of the lost child...

JACK: I've seen this footage before... it was smuggled out of Vacaville a couple of years ago... fast forward it.

>Bob fast forwards the tape, sending the image of Charlie into a comic, silent movie speed. Jack watches the image.

BOB: Maybe whoever sent this thinks you'll use it...

Leslie.

JACK (angry): Noooo way. I, the media has blitzed him already... every time there is a piece on the Family's murders, it's Charlie. Charlie, the pied piper of evil... they always ignore the kids who put the knives and bullets into the victims.

[INT. DAY – Prison C.I.W.]

LESLIE: Bobby and Gypsy and I... were sort of this traveling family of our own...

[INT. NIGHT – Prison San Quentin]

   Old Bobby, age 49, being interviewed for "Crime Scene".

BOBBY: I already had that shit down. When I met him, I had my girls, he had his.

[INT. NIGHT – Bobby's teepee]

   Inside of Bobby's teepee, getting stoned and tripping on acid are Leslie, Bobby and Sandra. The interior is very psychedelic, Bobby's art work awash in the glow of candles and a rotating lava lamp. Colors glide over the three, who sit cross legged around a large hookah pipe. Sandy takes a hit and passes the hose to Bobby while Leslie anxiously runs her hand through a

> bowl of Zuzus lying at her feet. Bobby is talking to Sandy, who looks stoned and completely humorless.

BOBBY: Your Daddy's rich, hunh...

SANDY: Very wealthy, San Diego stockbroker... it means nothing to me... he never gave me any love. The money, European vacations, college... he was trying to buy my love, my respect, approval and emotions...

> Leslie, who is tripping more heavily than Bobby or Sandy, is examining the skin of her left arm. She looks very distraught. We see her point of view. Moving in close to the skin, we see a volcano shaped welt that erupts in a shower of spark, flame and smoke. Green worms emerge from bleeding pores, wriggling obscenely. Leslie freaks out. She jumps, kicking the Zuzu bowl over.

LESLIE: My skin! AAAIIIEEE!! Bobby! Help me!!!

BOBBY: What's wrong?

LESLIE: Volcanoes! Volcanoes and worms on my skin!!! They're eating my skin!!! Help me!!!

> Bobby drops the hookah hose and moves over to Leslie.

BOBBY (grabbing her arm): Easy! Easy! Look... volcanoes are beautiful! Fire is beautiful!

> Leslie jerks free and disappears through a flap in the tarp.

LESLIE: I'm BURNING!!!

> Bobby follows her out into the night. Sandy watches them go while sucking on the hose.

[EXT. NIGHT – Outside of Bobby's teepee]

> With a full yellow moon hanging in the sky behind them, Bobby grabs Leslie by both arms and tries to soothe her.

LESLIE: AAAiiieeeuuunnnhhhhhhh.....

BOBBY: Stop it! Look at your skin, dammit! It's beautiful! See how beautiful it is? It's your love.

LESLIE: Bobby, I'm burning!!

BOBBY: Fire is your love! Don't fight it... Look, look at love.

LESLIE: I'm dying...

>   Bobby steps behind Leslie and holds her close, rocking her gently...

BOBBY: Let it die. Easy... easy, relax, Let it die.. let it go where it wants... let it go. Easy... Let it die and bring your love back. Feel your love coming back.....

>   Leslie, starting to calm somewhat, repeats Bobby's name like a mantra, softly.

LESLIE: Bobby... Bobby...

BOBBY: Don't let anyone into your head but me... No one but me... Give it to me... Be one with me... Give me your love...

>   Through a flood of tears, Leslie smiles weakly.

LESLIE: I – I hear the stars...

BOBBY: So do I...

LESLIE: They're singing...

BOBBY: Don't they sound beautiful?

[INT. DAY – Prison C.I.W.]

LESLIE: Bobby met Charlie...

[INT. NIGHT – Prison S.Q.]

BOBBY: If anybody was influenced, it was him, by me.

[INT. DAY – Prison C.I.W.]

LESLIE: ...and so I met Charlie.

[INT. DAY – Prison S.Q.]

BOBBY: Making music is how I met Charlie... when I joined a band, called the Milky Way. Charlie was in it. He was a fine musician, very intense, very vivid from being locked up all that time. And he was a great lyricist.

[INT. DAY – Office/Linda interview '71]

Linda and Patty.

LINDA: I was... like a lot of kids my age, looking for God. On a quest for God. Stumbling around, taking drugs, kind of like a blind girl in the forest.

[INT. TWILIGHT – Linda's dining room.]

>Sitting at a table, smoking a joint, are Patty and Linda. In a playpen beside Linda's chair is TANYA, her eight month old daughter.

LINDA: I never thought I'd see the day when Bob joined the establishment... it's just really fucked.

PATTY: Linda... it looks to me like you've grown apart.

LINDA: It's just that... things aren't the same.

>Linda reaches for the joint.

LINDA: Let me hit that now.

>In her playpen, Tanya stops playing with her rattle and looks over at her mother.

PATTY (V.O.): Linda... I want you to come to the ranch with me... just for a few days. [Pause] Charlie acts from his soul, because his ego is dead. It died a long time ago. No ego, just soul... And he's a great lover. Charlie is the man we've all been waiting for.

LINDA: I'll go... for a few days.

[INT. NIGHT – Documentary background/black cyclorama]

SNAKE: Before I met Charlie... I wasn't aware of how I was wasting my life. Living in an apartment, with my dog, my life was really routine. Go to work, go home, go shopping, go to work, go home, go shopping, it was really a drag. And then Charlie blew in and I just dropped it all, I just dropped everything and took off... He brought out all of these things that I was just sticking in slots...

[INT. NIGHT – Prison S.Q.]

BOBBY: When Charlie got out... he was 33, he'd been locked up since he was 13. And he was lonely, and this was the first time that he had a group of women that cared about him, that loved him, and Charlie loved those girls. He treated them with plenty of respect.

[INT. NIGHT – Prison San Luis Obispo]

> Tex, age 50, now a Church Deacon, being interviewed for "Crime Scene" in the Prison Chapel.

TEX: Well, I was trying to get close to Charlie's girls. It's astounding to me that Charlie even knew Dennis and we were all living in this rich rock star's mansion.

[CUT TO: Quick animation of Sadie and Patty, naked, against an orange background]

[EXT. DAY – The HOLLYWOOD sign.]

[INT. NIGHT – Prison S.L.O.]

TEX: But then Dennis wised up and kicked us all out.

[EXT. DAY – L.A. parking lot]

> Sadie kisses Tex.

SADIE: There is a lot of acid out at the ranch.

[INT. NIGHT – Prison S.L.O.]

Sadie and Patty.

TEX: I followed them out to the ranch and tried to integrate myself with Charlie. [Wincing] Umm... I guess you had to be there... I didn't really know how to perceive Charlie, but I knew I needed acceptance and love... And I wanted the responsibility-free lifestyle of the Family.

[EXT. DAY – An open field behind the Ranch]

> Charlie is rapping to Family members, gathered in a circle around him. In the distance, Tex is being led to the group by Sadie and Patty.

CHARLIE: And now I have to hide my soul or you will kill me... And that's why the kids have to hide; so they don't die...

BOBBY: Right on...

CHARLIE: Man... You come out and your parents say, "Shut up! Get back inside yourself. You don't need to be so bright, cause then we've got to judge ourselves." They hate to look at the truth in themselves, man.

> Tex, Sadie and Patty arrive. Sadie and Patty run up to Charlie and hug him.

CHARLIE: Hi Sadie...

Bobby, Brenda, Clem.

> The girls kneel down beside Charlie and give him warm, "we're home..." kisses.

SADIE: This is Tex. He wants to stay with us.

CHARLIE: I speak the will of God, son. You can have anything I got!

> Charlie rises and walks to Tex. Tex is nervous, but eager to please.

[INT. DAY – Documentary background/black cyclorama]

NANCY: Charlie wasn't the leader ...at all, he followed us around and took care of us.

[EXT. DAY – An open field outside the Ranch.]

> Charlie is confronting Tex in front of the rest of the Family members.

CHARLIE: Are you ready to die in the mind and live from the soul?

TEX (flustered): Sure... yeah...

CHARLIE: Have you accepted that we are all one?

TEX: Yeah... You know, yeah. I guess I have.

> Charlie becomes impassioned.

CHARLIE: There is no guess! The President guesses how many of our brothers should die across the ocean everyday.

PATTY: Amen, Charlie!

CHARLIE: The man guesses how many bullets to fire into a crowd of beautiful children. There is no guess.

> Charlie kneels in front of Tex and kisses his feet, making Tex distinctly uncomfortable.

PATTY: Far out...

> Charlie rises slowly, producing a large "Owsley White Lightning LSD-25" tablet from his pocket. He holds it before Tex's face. Tex has never tripped before.

CHARLIE: Are you ready to die?

Tex, Charlie.

    Tex removes his sunglasses.

TEX: Yes... I have...

    Charlie places the LSD-25 in Tex's mouth.

CHARLIE: Then live forever!

[INT. DAY – Office/Linda interview '71]

LINDA: Being accepted by the Family and Charlie was an answer... an answer to an unspoken prayer.

[EXT. DAY – Open field outside of Ranch]

    Charlie gives Tex a hug, then prances over to his guitar. The Family sings with Charlie. Tex is overwhelmed. Sadie kisses him as his trip intensifies.

[INT. DAY – Documentary footage/Sunshine]

    A very stoned SUNSHINE, with mustache, is talking to the camera in front of a black cyclorama.

SUNSHINE: Before his Helter Skelter trip... it was really beautiful. All we did was smoke grass, drop acid, and make love, as much as possible...

[INT. DAY – Office/Linda interview '71]

LINDA: We were forced to examine our souls... not privately, or secretly, but before Charlie and the entire Family.

[INT. DAY – Documentary footage/Sunshine]

SUNSHINE: Everything that everything was for, was for fucking. That's what everything was for, man...

[INT. DAY – Office/Linda interview '71]

LINDA: To unify ourselves through LSD...

[INT. DAY – Documentary footage/Sunshine]

SUNSHINE: I mean, if we weren't fucking, we were leading up to it.

[INT. DAY – Office/Linda interview '71]

LINDA: It was heavy.

[INT. DAY – Documentary footage/Sunshine]

SUNSHINE: And if we weren't leading up to it, we were fucking.

[EXT. DAY – Open field outside of Ranch]

> The Family begins a game where half of them support the weight of the other half while standing; the limp and formless members rolling against and off of the supporting members. Camera follows Tex as one of the formless rollers. The Family members stand in a circle, chanting a mantra, rising and falling in pitch and volume, and they approach the peak of their trip. Clothing is wrestled loosely from the bodies of all by the others, until all are naked and standing against another, grooving slowly to the rhythms of the trip.

[INT. DAY – Prison S.L.O.]

TEX: I didn't have any experience with group sex, but... I warmed up to it. The girls kept telling me, that it was my parents' hang ups, that I had to deprogram myself from their inhibitions.

[EXT. DAY – Open field outside of Ranch]

Family orgy.

As the twilight fills the open sky, the Family is nude and being prepared for an orgy by Charlie. Sadie leads Tex to a secluded spot and makes frantic love to him.

[INT. DAY – Documentary footage/Sunshine]

SUNSHINE: That's what Charlie said the whole universe was about, man... it was all one big fuck. Everything was in and out. Smoking, eating, drinking... it was all just one big fuck.

[INT. TWILIGHT – Linda's dining room]

PATTY: We're not Hippies... we're Slippies!

    The two girls laugh.

[EXT. DAY – Open field outside of Ranch]

    We see Charlie making love to Brenda. Nearby, a spider leaps from its web, leaving its eggs swing.

[EXT. DAY – Mountains/Ranch]

    Tex is in Voice Over, we see the mountains, then the Ranch owned by an eighty year old man, named George.

TEX (V.O.): Well, the ranch was fairly isolated. You had to take a back road from the Santa Susanna Pass to get there... and it was owned by this eighty year old, blind guy named George. Well, Charlie never really believed that George was completely blind, he would have one of the girls strip down in front of him from time to time, just to see if there was some sort of reaction. And Charlie was always trying to cultivate George with the girls, you know, to help cook and clean and make love to him. And of course we helped out around the ranch. Whatever, shoveling manure, grooming the horses, whatever it took to keep up a good front and make us look good with George. I don't think George was ever conned.

[MONTAGE – DOCUMENTARY FOOTAGE OF OLD GEORGE.]

[EXT. DAY – The Ranch]

> OLD GEORGE being helped out by Family girls, George out at the corral with Simi, Family, and drinking lemonade with Shorty on the front porch.

TEX (V.O.): And for the most part, we got along with the other ranch hands. Except for Shorty.

[EXT. DAY – Dirt road at the Ranch]

> A group of Family girls are blocking a pick up truck, making witchy symbols at the driver, Shorty, a ranch hand for Old George. Shorty screams at the girls and steps on it. He tears through, leaving a cloud of dust and the girls laughing.

SHORTY: Freaks!

> A young girl who occasionally helps Shorty with the horses, SIMI SHERRI, sees Shorty's truck pull up. Shorty parks and gets out of the truck, drunk, holding a whiskey bottle. He sees Simi and tries to hide it.

[INT. DAY – Prison S.L.O.]

TEX: Charlie tried, but Shorty was just the one Ranch hand that he couldn't work his magic on.

[INT. DAY – Prison C.I.W.]

> Patty, age 49, is being interviewed for "Crime Scene".

PATTY: And what people refuse to understand is that Charlie wasn't looking for attention. Which is why he got so much of it.

Patty.

[EXT. DAY. – Path beside the old barn/Ranch]

    Simi, carrying Shorty's chaps, walks past a barn, from wherein the sounds of lovemaking can be heard. She steps up on a pile of logs to peer through the slats of the barn. She sees Sadie, Patty and Bobby inside the barn, engaged in sex. The log slips, Simi loses her balance and falls onto a large metal container. Sadie, Patty, and Bobby stop and look toward the noise. Simi gets up, embarrassed, and grabs the chaps.

SIMI: Sorry.....

    Sadie giggles at Simi.

[EXT. DAY – Horse corral/Ranch]

    Shorty is leading the horses from the corral to the stables. Tex is following him, blabbering on about his defunct wig business.

SHORTY: Just get the gate for me, will you...

TEX: Sure.

    Tex undoes the gate latch and Shorty leads the horse through.

SHORTY (to horse): C'mon... Okay.

> Tex rejoins Shorty and the horse.

TEX: I'm not bullshitting you, man. You know, you come to me with these wigs, you know, we're going to make a lot of money together. It's just a small investment on your part.

> Simi walks up to Tex and Shorty, carrying Shorty's chaps.

SIMI: So Tex... is umm... is uh, Sadie your girlfriend?

TEX: Well, yes, we were supposed to go swimming this morning... Have you seen her?

SIMI: You two sure have weird concepts of "boyfriend/girlfriend"...

TEX: What's that supposed to mean? Do you know where she is?

SIMI: Yeah. She's in the old barn, over by the stables... but... she wasn't exactly alone...

> Tex looks at Simi with uncertainty. He then walks toward the old barn. Shorty watches Tex wander off.

SHORTY: What's going on, Simi?

SIMI: Aren't we nosey?

> The horse flicks its tail in Shorty's face. Simi laughs and throws Shorty's chaps at him.

SIMI: Here's your plastic bullshit chaps.

SHORTY: Whad'ya mean, PLASTIC?

SIMI: You think you're a movie star?

SHORTY: Yeah... I will be... you wait and see!

SIMI: Oh... okay.

> Simi giggles at Shorty.

[INT. DAY – Old barn by the stables/Ranch]

> Tex opens the door slowly. He sees Patty getting dressed. He pushes the door open and sees Bobby and Sadie at the far

end of the barn, half undressed. They are smoking a joint. Tex walks toward them. Patty sees him and approaches him warily.

PATTY: Hi Tex...

Tex continues and stands over Sadie and Bobby.

SADIE: Hi Tex...

TEX: Sadie... I've been looking for you all morning... What've you been doing?

SADIE: Tripping... and balling...

Bobby laughs at this.

SADIE: All morning long. You should get up earlier, Tex. [Pause] What's the problem?

TEX: Goddammit, Sadie. Last night, you said that we were going swimming this morning. I didn't know you were going to be in the barn, fucking Bobby.

SADIE: Look, I don't belong to you Tex, you got that? I don't belong to anybody. I can do whatever I want and so can you.

TEX: Then why in the Hell did you bring me here in the first place?

SADIE: I brought you here to meet everyone... I brought you here to meet Charlie.

TEX: CHARLIE... CHARLIE... CHARLIE... That's all I fucking hear. What has Charlie got to do with anything? How in the Hell did Charlie get to be KING SHIT?!!

SADIE: Because Charlie has all the love... Everybody has given all of their love to Charlie.

Sadie begins kissing and groping Bobby.

TEX: You slut.

BOBBY: Get out of here!

[INT. DAY – Prison S.L.O.]

TEX: I didn't know what to make of Bobby when I met him. He seemed like a spoiled, super hippie, you know? Arrogant, always trying to use a power that he really didn't have, to influence the rest of the group.

[INT. NIGHT – Documentary footage/Squeaky and Gypsy]

SQUEAKY: Charlie wasn't our leader. He didn't want us hanging on him, like our parents wanted us hanging on them.

GYPSY: We didn't need them.

SQUEAKY: Charlie let us be beautiful.

[INT. DAY – Prison S.L.O.]

TEX: Sometimes our group lovemaking was comical, other times it was devastating. But that's how we were growing. We were forming a bond as a family. And Charlie was directing all these energies... but no one could direct them.

[EXT. DAY – Waterfall and stream near Ranch.]

> Several members of the Family are tripping and skinny dipping in a stream. Sadie flirts with Tex, who sits nude in a tree. He smiles at her.

[DISSOLVE]

[EXT. TWILIGHT – The Ranch]

> Members of the Family sit around a fire, playing musical instruments.

PATTY: I'm willing to die for Charlie, because he's me... we're all one soul.

[INT. DAY – Prison S.L.O.]

TEX: Well, we believed that we were cleansing ourselves, spiritually. The goal was to achieve an inner harmony... as a group, as an example to the rest of the world, which we saw as phoney and desperate.

[INT. NIGHT – Documentary footage/Squeaky and Gypsy]

SQUEAKY: We talk this way about Charlie and people, like you, say that we're brainwashed. But we've seen Charlie do things that no human being has done before. We saw him pick up a bird in the desert and breath on it and bring it back to life.

[INT. DAY – Prison C.I.W.]

> Sadie, age 48, is being interviewed for "Crime Scene".

SADIE: And he said, "See? I told you that you were perfect. You must always think of yourself as perfection." ...and I bought it and him and the whole brainwash.

[EXT. DAY – A hill and stream beside the Ranch]

> Sadie walks down the hill in a huff. Tex runs behind, following her. Sadie sees Charlie and CLEM, smoking a bowl, beside the stream. She walks up to them as Tex catches up to her.

SADIE: Hi, you guys.

CLEM: Hello Sadie.

SADIE: Clem, I really need to hit that bowl...

> Clem gives her the pipe.

CLEM: Go ahead... But I think it's cooked.

> Sadie is upset.

SADIE: Charlie! Clem! This isn't fair. Man, I've been trying to get a buzz off of everybody. Nobody has nothing.

CLEM: Awww....

SADIE: Clem! I need to get high. Pack me a bowl.

CLEM: That was the last one...

SADIE: You've got to be kidding...

CLEM: There isn't any more.

> Sadie stands up as Charlie and Clem laugh.

SADIE: No! No! Goddammit! Goddammit, Charlie! I think that sucks!

CHARLIE: Hmmm... Yeah?..

SADIE: We should have never left the Spiral Staircase. At least they always had a steady supply of drugs! Maybe I should go back and live with them.

> Tex grabs Sadie's shoulders.

TEX: I know where we can get some dope, some killer weed, a lot of it, maybe a pound. I've got some connections.

Charlie, Tex, Sadie.

SADIE: Give me some money, Charlie. Me and Tex are going to go get the dope.

CHARLIE: We're out of money, honey.

> Clem and Charlie laugh again.

SADIE: Goddammit Charlie, I think that sucks! You make me sick, sometimes! You're so goddamn selfish, you don't care about anyone, but yourself.

TEX: Hey, we don't need money. I know some knuckleheads I can burn for at least a lid. C'mon, let's go.

> As Sadie and Tex begin to walk away, Charlie reaches out and grabs Sadie's leg.

CHARLIE: Hey, whoa, Sadie!

SADIE: Charlie! Charlie, let go of my leg.

> Sadie falls to the ground and struggles.

CHARLIE: Hold the door, Sadie! Hold on, now. You crazy woman, you done got me all dirty again. You've got some dirty feet here, Sadie. Let's clean them! C'mon Sadie. Let's clean these feet here.

> Amidst her protest, Charlie drags Sadie to the stream by her foot. Sadie quiets as Charlie softly cleans her foot in the cool water. Tex grudgingly sits down behind Sadie. Suddenly, Charlie stops and removes a joint from his back pocket. Sadie falls back into Tex.

SADIE: A joint! You've got... You've got pot! Charlie has a joint. Thank God!

CHARLIE (extending the joint): Would you light this, Tex?

[INT. DAY – Prison S.L.O.]

TEX: There was a love there. A very strong, very true love there. And if I hadn't felt it, I never would have followed Charlie.

[INT. DAY – Back of a city Metro bus]

> Alone, playing with small figurines of circus animals, sits Stevie. He is riding the bus. He looks out of the window, bored. Suddenly inspired, he removes a ski mask from his pocket and puts it on his face. He is now the Crimson Avenger!

[INT. DAY – J. Wilson's VPP suite]

> Bob stops the Charlie videotape, and ejects it.

JACK: Who do you think sent that?

BOB: Probably a practical joke from some kids.

JACK: Charlie has become a sick, underground hero to some of these kids... wait a minute...

> Jack stands and grabs a poster tube. He removes the poster.

JACK: I meant to show this to you when I came in. I bought this yesterday at the Dark Fantasy Comic Book Store... the poster is rows upon rows of Charlie faces...

BOB: That's great... should we get back to work?

> Jack puts the poster away.

[INT. EARLY MORNING – Ranch house]

> Patty, Ouisch, Stephanie, Catherine, and Snake are sewing. Patty and Ouisch are putting the finishing touches on a long

> black cape for Charlie, while the others are embroidering his vest. Patty is relating her thoughts about yesterday's acid trip.

PATTY: And just when I started peaking... I looked over and Charlie said, "Now... you're perfect. Then I knew... and I knew he knew that he's right. I mean... I could remember all the different lives I've lived, all the different bodies over the centuries. I know now that it's all been leading up to right now. All the living, all the dying, all the coming back over and over and over and over. But this is the last time. Like, the way I feel... It's like everyone in the Family. We've come up from millions of years and now we're all perfect. I've got exactly the body I wanted, you know, for the last time. The strongest and most perfect... the one that's gonna make it through for the last time. I'm willing to die for Charlie, 'cause he's me... we're all one soul.

STEPHANIE: That's right... it's coming down fast...

> Sadie enters and sits with the girls. She searches through a cigar box for some dope, as she speaks.

SADIE: Did you see Brenda? She looks like someone beat the shit out of her. Charlie, again?

OUISCH: It was at dinner last night... where were you, Sadie?

SADIE: I was out on the Strip with Bobby.

STEPHANIE: You know that Soul wants everybody together for dinner.

SADIE: Sometimes, I don't give a shit, all right? What happened?

CATHERINE: Charlie's getting pissed at you, Sadie! If you bring the clap back with you one of these days...

SADIE: What happened to Brenda?

PATTY: She just wanted some attention, like she always does... so she angered the Devil.

OUISCH: She waited until Charlie was talking to all of us, then she started talking to Clem.

STEPHANIE: So, Charlie threw a bowl of rice at her head.

CATHERINE: He did more than that...

> Sadie is sick of hearing about Charlie. She really wants to get high. She removes an empty baggy from the cigar box.

Catherine, Patty.

SADIE: Is this all the grass we got?

    Patty stands and models the cape for the other girls.

PATTY: This is gonna look groovy on Soul...

SADIE: Where's all the grass we had?

PATTY: There was only a couple of joints left, Sadie...

    Ouisch grabs up a tiny roach from the dirt floor.

OUISCH: Here's a roach....

    Sadie tosses the roach to the ground and storms out.

SADIE: Thanks a fucking lot for saving me some!

    The girls watch her go and giggle amongst themselves, stoned.

CATHERINE: She's the biggest bitch... if she gives us the clap, I swear I'll kick her ass!

[EXT. DAY – Porch of saloon at Ranch]

Pooh Bear, Cappy, Lil' Patty, Snake.

>Some Family girls play with the children, Pooh Bear and Zezozoze.

SADIE (V.O.): Charlie told us that children were the real leaders of the Family. They were the ones that lead the way. Since we waited on them, they set the pace.

[INT. DAY – Documentary background/black cyclorama]

NANCY: Jesus Christ and his children were just kids. They were living free, without guilt and without shame. They were able to take off their clothes and lie in the sun and be one together.

[INT. DAY – Prison S.L.O.]

TEX: We took hundreds of acid trips together, smoked a lot of pot together... because we wanted to be like Charlie, because to us... he was living perfection. We wanted to mirror him.

[EXT. DAY – Death Valley]

>A small number of Family members are tripping, nude, under the huge desert sky. They are oblivious to everything. We see Tex coupled with Sadie. They are one mind, for the time being.

Mars, Dennis.

[INT. DAY – J. Wilson's VPP suite]

    We see the old Sadie, speaking form a video monitor.

SADIE (on screen): We had so much sex... every kind! It's a miracle that I'm not dead from diseases. I had no standards... I'd sleep with anybody. Anybody I wanted to sleep with or anyone Charlie asked me to sleep with. He'd always give me to the meanest biker or the craziest whoever. He knew I could outfreak anybody with sex and he used me and my body to smooth out problems. I see AIDS as something God created, to monitor such unhealthy lifestyles.

    Sadie's face freezes on the monitor. Jack sits back in his chair.

JACK: When the Family went on trial... It's just one of those milestones in the death of the Hippie movement... like Patty Hearst and....

[INT. DAY – Basement of Mars' house]

    Dennis, Mars, Lucy and Stevie are gathered in a dirty, but decorated basement. They hang out here. They are nude. Dennis sits at a table, doing lines of cocaine. Before him, magically, appears a floating .32 revolver. He reaches out, like MacBeth and his dagger. Dennis grabs the handgun and stares at it with intense admiration. The room's sound is dominated by the steady crackle of an electrical Jacob's Ladder and the booming voice of Jim Jones.

REV. JIM JONES (V.O.): Martin Luther King died talking about love! Kennedy died, talking about something he couldn't even understand, some kind of generalized love and he never even backed it up! He sucked out! Bullshit! Love is the only weapon with which I've got to fight? I've got a Hell of a lot of weapons to fight! I've got my clothes, I've got compasses, I got guns, I got dynamite, I've got a Hell of a lot to fight! I'll fight! I'll FIGHT! I'm telling you to stop this now, if you have any respect at all. Are we Black, Proud, Socialists, or what are we?

> Dennis looks down at the .32 bullets resting on the mirror in front of him.

[INT. DAY – J. Wilson's VPP suite]

BOB: If only Charlie had become a rock star...

JACK: That's another thing... the bookstore where I got the poster, they had for sale Charlie's two albums! Available on vinyl and CD.

> Bob lights a cigarette.

BOB: He finally made the record bins...

JACK: It's ridiculous...

BOB: Did you buy them?

JACK: I didn't have my checkbook with me.

[INT. NIGHT – BBC music talk show/black and white]

> An older, bearded TERRY, Charlie's would-be record producer, is being interviewed by the show's host, IAN.

IAN: So, Terry, what was it like to talk to Charlie?

TERRY: You could take him in very small doses, I mean... he'd throw ten things at you... you'd be on three, he'd be on seven and getting real physical about it. He'd bend over, pick up a handful of rocks and toss them into the air and say, "See, you can throw it all away and it'll come back to you." [Laughs]

[EXT. DAY – Outside of Universal Recording]

> Terry is talking to Charlie as he unlocks the studio door.

CHARLIE (realizing Greg's absence): Greg was supposed to come with you, wasn't he?

TERRY (lying): Umm, he called right before I left to get him. He's pretty sick, I guess.

CHARLIE: Sick?

TERRY: We can get by without him, don't worry.

CHARLIE: It's like the man, dig? It's society and your parents programming us right from the start... programming us all with the garbage on TV; to wear these clothes and buy this car and all the things that are polluting this earth. You see it in all the young love programmed to go to war. To hate gooks and kill 'em in the name of liberty or the flag or whatever... But the child is beautiful, perfect... so his reaction is to that, is to run, you know? To hide himself... It's not a hard thing to see. We're flashing with divine harmony this morning. I just wrote two songs while the sun was rising.

TERRY: Very... very, groovy.

> Terry lets the screen door slam on Charlie.

[INT. DAY – Prison C.I.W.]

JACK W: Charlie was basically screwed over by the recording executives. Am I right?

PATTY: I don't know what you're talking about.

JACK W: Well, the legend is that Charlie was frustrated by his lack of success in the music business, so he turned to murder.

PATTY: That couldn't be farther from the truth.

JACK W: Tell me the truth, Patty.

PATTY: Charlie was not willing to sell out to the producers and that's the FIRST and most important requirement before the industry is willing to handle an artist.

[INT. DAY – Universal Recording]

> Terry watches through the window of the control room as his recording engineer, J.T., is engaged in a heated argument with Patty, Sadie, Bobby and Charlie inside the studio. J.T. is yelling to be heard over the bickering.

J.T: I need you in the booth and them out here! Okay! If it's shit you want... Fine! 'Cause that's what you're gonna get with a one mike set-up. Now, if you want professional sound, maybe something you can use, I suggest you get in the booth and leave the rest to me!

> Terry enters the studio to break up the fight.

TERRY: Hey, hey, hey! What's the problem here?!

[INT. DAY – C.I.W.]

PATTY: Many musicians say they don't care about the money, yet they commit themselves to appear at given times and places and to produce what sells, whether they believe in it or not. Charlie didn't want to be imprisoned. He wanted success on his own terms.

[INT. DAY – Universal Recording]

> Charlie is arguing with Terry and J.T., as Bobby, Sadie and Patty watch.

CHARLIE: If our message is going to get across, we have to be able to do our own thing, goddammit!

J.T: Good. Do your own thing! Fuck him.

> J.T. storms for the door, but is stopped by Terry.

TERRY: Wait, Jerry. C'mon, whoa, whoa, hey, c'mon Charlie. Be sensible. This is the way that all groups do it. Dennis would tell you.

CHARLIE: Where the Hell is Dennis?

TERRY: I tried to call him, man.

CHARLIE: Why don't you try calling him again, I want to talk to Dennis.

TERRY: Wait a second, wait a second here, Charlie. You want the best sound, right?

CHARLIE: I want MY sound.

TERRY: Bobby, you've been in the studio before, right?

BOBBY: Right, with the Powerhouse...

CHARLIE (cuts Bobby off): I know what's best for us! I know!

BOBBY: I just think we need something more organic, that's all I'm saying.

J.T: Do you know anything about the acoustics in this studio? Do you know anything about EQ? Do you know anything about mixing? Do you know any of that stuff...?

BOBBY: I know a little bit about...

CHARLIE: I know about the Energy Rays of a Free Love Society and I know your cold, heartless technology hasn't defined that yet.

PATTY/SADIE: Amen, Charlie.

CHARLIE: But it's there. It's here...

    Charlie slaps his head, repeatedly.

CHARLIE: .....in a thought, it's in a thought, it's in a thought from me to you.

    Charlie strikes out with his palm, hitting J.T. in the forehead.

J.T: I don't have to take this shit!

TERRY: Charlie! What are you doing? You don't go around slapping people! We need him! Goddammit!

Terry, Charlie, Bobby, Patty, Sadie.

CHARLIE: But Terry...

TERRY: No, no, no buts. No buts, Charlie.

    Bobby re-enters the studio.

BOBBY: He ain't coming back, man.

TERRY: C'mon really, man. I told you I'd do the best for you that I could, okay?

SADIE: Well, fuck you and your bullshit studio!

TERRY: Hey! Is that... is that what you think, man?

PATTY: Charlie does things his way, he don't conform to the pig rules of the establishment.

[INT. NIGHT – BBC music talk show]

IAN: So, Terry, you worked in the studio with Charlie... Now, you're his producer. What did you think of him, as a musician, as an artist?

TERRY: Charlie was at the edge. Just the whole Sixties scene, L.A., things kind of built to a critical mass and at one point, I actually thought, 'Well, maybe there's something we could do with this...' ...but...

IAN: But the music was really crap, wasn't it?

> The studio audience laughs.

TERRY (chuckling): Yes... the music was crap.

> The audience roars.

IAN: We're so formal over here, on the BBC.

[INT. NIGHT – Universal Recording]

> Charlie is recording one of his compositions inside of a small booth, while Terry watches anxiously from behind a large window. Beside Terry sits a grumbling J.T., who records Charlie on tape.

[INT. NIGHT – Prison S.Q.]

BOBBY: I mean, things looked good for Charlie ...and everybody was just goofing with their heads in the clouds.

[EXT. DAY – The Ranch]

> We see various Family members enjoying the sunshine, playing with children, smoking pot, kissing and play acting.

TEX (V.O.): Well, we gave up our birthdays and renounced our families. Charlie didn't allow any clocks, calendars or anything like that on the ranch. Dennis and Bobby were donating food, cars, whatever. It was always submit. Give something to Charlie, submit everything you had. Submit your ego. That whole summer seems like a dream.

> Sandy, Patty and Squeaky are enacting "The Perils of Pauline", for the amusement of the other Family girls. Patty wraps Sandy with a rope.

SQUEAKY: If you do not give us the deed to the ranch, I will throw you on the railroad track! AHAAHHAAAHAHAHA!!

SANDY: Help! Save me, Save me!

> Squeaky curls her non-existent mustache.

Shorty.

[INT. NIGHT – Prison S.Q.]

BOBBY: We'd just drop acid and share out of this big pile of clothes and costumes... and role play the day away. Changing situations and characters.

[EXT. DAY – The Ranch]

> Cappy is wearing a green demon mask. She rips it off and laughs like a mad hatter. Bobby walks to Nancy, with Snake and Lil' Patty on his arms. He kneels before Nancy, opens his mouth and sticks out his tongue, revealing two hits of powerful blotter acid. He laughs.

[EXT. DAY – Horse corral/Ranch]

> Shorty is in a heated argument with Patty and other Family girls, who are perched on the corral fence, passing a joint amongst themselves.

SHORTY: Well, you're all going to be clearing out of here pretty soon, because Old George is getting real tired of you giving this ranch a bad name.

KITTY: That's not what Mary says....

SHORTY: Mary doesn't know shit from beans... I'm George's right hand man and I know what he's thinking.

OUISCH: We'll see about that..

BO: The karma is turning, Shorty. The karma is turning.

SHORTY: I don't understand all you little creeps... Charlie's not Jesus Christ, he's not the Devil. He's just a little con man... He's spent half his life in prison, goddammit!

>Patty laughs at Shorty.

[INT. DAY – Prison S.L.O.]

JACK W: The ranch then became headquarters for a car theft ring, as well as for the breaking and entering...

TEX: Charlie was bringing bikers out to the ranch, I was kept busy at that time... We'd steal cars, mostly Volkswagens, tear them apart and build dune buggies or sell the parts. Shorty started watching us closer and after a while, became a problem for Charlie.

JACK: How was Shorty a problem?

TEX: Like I said... He started watching us real close, keeping track of everything we brought onto the ranch.

[STILL PHOTOGRAPHS/MONTAGE]

>Black and white photographs of Shorty, posing with his wife, Denise, are shown over the following interview with Tex.

TEX (V.O.): Charlie convinced Juan and Clem, who were ranch hands, to join the Family, but never Shorty. He was too much of an outsider. He was also married to this black go-go dancer, which was a "sin" in Charlie's eyes. Charlie's a racial bigot.

[EXT. DAY – Field outside stables/the Ranch]

>Stoned, Bobby and Clem are approaching the stables to taunt Shorty. Bobby is firing the Family's .22 Buntline revolver into the trees, for added menace.

CLEM (yelling): Shorty! You nigger lover! I heard your wife takes it up the ass, is that true?

BOBBY (yelling): Shorty!

Clem and Bobby.

    Shorty appears at the doorway, unfazed. He spits, then turns away in disgust. Clem and Bobby come running toward him.

[EXT. DAY – Outside of the stables/the Ranch horse corral]

    Patty laughs at Shorty.

PATTY: Loose lips sink ships...

[INT. DAY – Office/Linda interview '71]

LINDA: He never said he was Christ... but he would imply. Like, when he'd look at me and smile and say, "Don't you know who I am?"

[EXT. TWILIGHT – Field beside old barn/Ranch]

PATTY: Charlie said, "You shouldn't speak English to them in the first year, just baby talk."

SADIE: Yeah, but I think that's kind of ridiculous, I mean... Charlie has some pretty stupid ideas sometimes. I started talking right away to Zezozoze.... But it's not bad though...

PATTY (half-pissed): What?

Ouisch and Patty.

SADIE: You know... Baby talk. Frek-Leka-Frekee-a-Lekka-Lekka...

    Patty and Linda crack up, laughing. Then the laughter dies out.

LINDA: I made love to Charlie last night.

SADIE: Yeah? How was it?

LINDA: It was...

PATTY: C'mon..

SADIE: Like... what was it like?

LINDA: It was great. It was kind of scary... He said all these really nice things to me... Then when he started to come... he got real tense. Then he climaxed and I came, but... I got all tense, it was like I couldn't move my arms... for about a minute... at all. I was paralyzed. It was real scary... I felt real cold.

PATTY: That's because your ego was dying. That's good! That's great! Because until it's dead... you can't give of yourself completely to anyone. That's why you couldn't move... It was rough. But you know what? Until you give of yourself completely and your ego's dead, you can't be at the Now. See what I'm saying? But it happens, you know...

Mars and Lucy.

[INT. DAY – Basement of Mars' house]

>Lucy is cooking up some heroin in a spoon, over a candle flame. A pentagram is visible on her stomach; a very poor branding. Mars sits on the steps, awaiting the injection. The Jim Jones Recording drones on.

REV. JIM JONES (V.O.): Stop this nonsense. You're exciting your children. No sorrow. I'm glad it's over. Hurry, hurry my children, hurry. It's an act of suicide, an act of revolutionary suicide.

MARS: We are now at the end of reason.

>Lucy has prepared the syringe. She stands and walks to Mars. Stevie sees them and begins itching. Scratching. Lucy shoots Mars up. Mars relaxes, Stevie scratches.

STEVIE: We are motion itself. We are eternal revolution.

[INT. NIGHT – Documentary footage/Gypsy interview]

>An angry Gypsy is holding a rifle, in front of a black cyclorama.

GYPSY: Yeah. He is God. That's why they're killing him! That's why they're sending him to the gas chamber!

[CUT TO: Squeaky, Gypsy and Sandy sit on a table in their matching fur collared denim vests, all three have rifles]

SQUEAKY: We saw him yell, "Die!", at a biker, until the biker crumbled into the dust and then Charlie restored him by yelling, "LIVE!"!!

[INT. NIGHT – The horse stables/the Ranch]

> Simi Sherri is having an upsetting conversation with Shorty, who is sitting on a table next to her. He is quite drunk. A half-empty bottle of Jack Daniel's lies in his lap.

SHORTY: You know, I've never told you... I... really like you.

SIMI: Goddamn you, Shorty! Why'd you drink all that for?

SHORTY: I'm really fond of you, Simi. We ought to get along better.

SIMI: How in the Hell am I supposed to get home now?

SHORTY: I'll take you home...

SIMI: You won't take me home! If you get behind the wheel, you'll kill us both! Now give me the keys. I'll be back in the morning.

SHORTY: No. No. No, I'll take us home. C'mon, have a drink...

> Shorty offers the bottle. Simi grabs it in a fit of anger.

SIMI: I got to go home! Thanks for nothing!

> Simi throws the bottle at the floor and storms off. Shorty calls, drunkenly, after her.

SHORTY: Hey... hey. I love you...

> Simi stops and yells back at Shorty.

SIMI: You're married, remember?!

> Simi continues walking, breaking into tears. She opens a door, revealing Tex rolling a joint inside the next room. Simi stops in her tracks.

SIMI: Sorry...

> Simi closes the door and turns back. She begins crying out of frustration and has to sit down.

[INT. DAY – Prison C.I.W.]

SADIE: Tex was trying to please Charlie, I think. Charlie loved it when somebody suddenly brought a new girl in. Sunshine was always bringing in girls to meet Charlie. Bobby would too, every now and then. I think Tex thought of Simi as a gift, more or less.

[INT. NIGHT – The horse stables]

> Simi is sitting down, crying. Tex opens the door and sees her.

TEX: Hey... Simi. What's the matter?

SIMI (sniffing): Nothing.

> Tex offers Simi the joint.

TEX: Do you want some of this?

SIMI (shaking her head): Hunh-uh.

TEX: It'll make you feel better.

SIMI: No, I don't want any. I, I don't have any way to get home. Shorty was supposed to take me and he got drunk. He gets drunk everyday, I work all day while he sits around and drinks. He was going to take me home 'cause my Mom is sick and I have to be home with her.

> Tex suddenly grabs Simi's boots and pulls them off.

SIMI: What are you doing?

TEX: You've been on these feet all day. I'm going to give them a massage.

> Tex begins massaging Simi's feet.

SIMI: Please... Stop...

TEX: Hey, I'll take you home, I'll take you home. Don't worry about it. I'll get the keys to the bread truck from Charlie.

SIMI: You're really crazy. Stop!

> Tex laughs at this.

Simi.

TEX: Yeah, I'm crazy. That's 'cause I care about you.

    Simi stops crying.

SIMI: Okay, enough. Go get the keys from Charlie.

TEX: Only if you promise... to come to a party with me.

SIMI: What party?

TEX: We throw parties here all the time. Everybody wants to meet you. Just come to this one. Okay?

[INT. NIGHT – Prison S.Q.]

BOBBY: Terry was supposed to come in and record us, in our natural environment. Charlie thought a record deal was coming too. When I showed up, the ranch was in full swing.

[INT. DAY – Prison S.L.O.]

TEX: Yeah, we had high expectations. Charlie had us clean the place from top to bottom. We had zuzus, hundreds of joints rolled. And the girls, well, they prepared this outstanding vegetarian feast.

PATTY (V.O.): The food those stores would throw away was perfectly good, and we only took the best of what was there.

[EXT. DAY – Trash dumpsters/supermarket]

> Family girls searching through garbage in a large bin, behind a supermarket.

SNAKE (V.O.): The first day I came to the ranch, Charlie sent me on a garbage run. He said, "Take some clean clothes, 'cause you'll get all dirty." And so I went down to the market and I hopped in the can, and we went through everything and we took it and cleaned it and took the skins off and cut all the spots out. Nobody goes hungry here.....

SADIE: We can't eat this shit. There's not enough for all of us. This is fucking disgusting. They never leave us anything good.

BO: Hey Sadie, Crawford's always has good rolls and breads. Their bakery throws out Tuesdays, Thursdays, Saturdays...

SADIE: Yeah, I know, but those places are so far away.

BO: Yeah...

SADIE: It just... doesn't make sense that we don't have connections here, since it is the closest.

PATTY: No sense makes sense.

[INT. DAY – Ranch house]

> Bo, Stephanie, Ouisch, Linda, Patty and Sadie are laying out a feast for record producer Terry M. Clem walks up to the feast and begins nibbling. He extends a lit joint to the girls.

STEPHANIE (grabbing the joint): I hope I'll be awake later with all of this.

BO: Make it good, you guys. Charlie really wants to make a good impression on this guy.

[INT. DAY – Record producer Terry's office]

> Terry is sitting behind his office desk, smoking a cigarette and talking on the phone to a very angry Charlie.

TERRY: Charlie, I'm sorry, man. I'm sorry I couldn't make it. I was... I was tied up in a meeting, okay? Hey.. Hey whoa, Charlie, Charlie, ease up man. I never promised you I'd be there. I said I'd come if I could, okay? Yeah. It's like I tried to explain to you before, the record execs don't think your stuff is marketable... right now. What I suggest that we do is, we'll sit on it until spring and who knows, by then you could be the biggest name since Jim Morrison. Whoa...whoa...whoa. What do you mean, "Make up my mind"? Charlie, I am not going to give up all my possessions and come live with you, man.

>Charlie hangs up on Terry. Terry hangs up.

TERRY: Little freak...

[INT. DAY – Prison Vacaville]

JACK W: And the record executives?

CHARLIE: Hell, those guys are better con men than anybody I ever met in prison.

[INT. DAY – Ranch house]

>Charlie, angered by Terry and the recordist not showing, goes berserk in front of the Family, destroying the vegetarian feast with his sword.

CHARLIE: Nobody cares about the music! AAAARRRGHH! Nobody cares! Nobody cares about the music!

[INT. DAY – Prison S.Q.]

BOBBY: It was a blow. I wanted that album to fly as much as Charlie. But I knew that, hey, it's all good. It's all music. So we rolled some joints and rolled with the punches.

JACK W: What do you mean it's all good? How do you differentiate between good and bad?

BOBBY: Good and bad? It's all good. Otherwise it wouldn't have happened. It's the way life flows, moves together.. I move with it. I don't question it.

[INT. NIGHT – BBC music talk show]

TERRY: This one little space in time, when Charlie was there... but he wasn't there.

[INT. DAY – Prison S.L.O.]

TEX: Charlie felt betrayed. His album was going to make us rich and spread his message to the world.

[INT. NIGHT – Prison S.Q.]

BOBBY: I mean, it didn't slow us down. We had all the makings for a great party.

[INT. DAY – Documentary footage/Sunshine]

SUNSHINE: When Simi came to the Family... She was a virgin and she was SCARED. She was scared stiff. [Pause] On her first experience with the Family, she was on mescaline. No wait, she was on acid, yeah, that's right. We had all taken acid that night, and uh... She flipped plum out, on that trip. She flipped completely out.

[INT. NIGHT – The horse stables/Ranch]

> Simi is smoking a joint with Bobby, Sadie and Tex, much to Shorty's disgust.

SHORTY: I'm very disappointed in you, Simi.

SIMI: Quit being such a drag, Shorty. Who are you to judge me? How many mornings have you come in smelling like booze and hung over and you can't do anything, until you've had your coffee, hunh?

> Tex rises, walks over to Shorty, grabs him by the shoulders and slams him against a stable door. He cups Shorty's frightened face in his hands.

TEX: You've got to die in the mind for your soul. For the sake of your soul. Free the mind and your ass is bound to follow, you dig, man?

SHORTY (bitter): Bully gets all the marbles.

> Tex walks back to Simi, Sadie and Bobby and sits down. Simi becomes uneasy in Shorty's absence.

TEX (to Simi): Charlie's real hip to you becoming a member of the Family.

SIMI: I didn't say I was going to join. I think Charlie's kind of scary, you guys.

> Sadie runs her hand through Simi's hair.

SADIE: But he's a great lover.

> Bobby fishes through his pockets and removes a piece of blotter acid.

TEX: Charlie's about the hippest guy I've ever met. He's going to open doors in this little brain of yours.

    Bobby holds up the blotter.

BOBBY: So will this.

SIMI: What's that?

BOBBY: This is LSD...

    He rips a small section off.

BOBBY: Here... Take two. We've already dropped. The whole Family's tripping tonight.

SIMI: I've never done any hard drugs before.

TEX: Break on through...

SADIE: It's not a hard drug. We don't do any hard drugs.

BOBBY: Come on. This is just blotter.

SADIE: It's just acid. It's not like it's heroin or cocaine or anything.

TEX: Break on through...

SADIE: It's a groove.

BOBBY: Come on, you're going to feel out of place if you don't take it.

SIMI: I don't know how.

BOBBY: What'd you mean, you don't know how? It's just like going to the doctor's office. Stick out your tongue and say, "Ah." Say, "Ah".

TEX: Break on through...

SIMI: Well... I have always wondered... what it's like, you know, to trip...

    Bobby turns to Sadie.

BOBBY: Say, "Ah".

SADIE: Ahhh...

> Bobby puts the acid on Sadie's tongue and rips some more off for Tex.

BOBBY: Say, "Ah".

TEX: Ahhh...

> Bobby places the blotter on Tex's tongue. He then rips some more off for Simi.

SADIE: Mmmm. Your turn.

TEX: Trust me...

BOBBY: Come on. It's a groove... Say, "Ah... Ahhh".

> Simi opens her mouth for the acid.

SIMI: Ahhh...

> Bobby promptly places the acid on her tongue.

[INT. NIGHT – Prison S.Q.]

BOBBY: Yeah, I remember that night, so what? We were tripping. She was too. We were all tripping right along and we balled our brains out, so what? It was good.

JACK W: She claimed later that it was rape.

BOBBY: That's her story. She was into it.

[INT. NIGHT – Ranch saloon]

> Through a series of distorted angles, unnerving sounds and disturbing images, it is conveyed that Simi is being raped against her will by the entire Family.

[INT. DAY – Documentary footage/Sunshine]

SUNSHINE: Everybody was doing their thing and she'd get all uptight and scared. And she'd fight and she's fighting and fighting and then she'd calm down and go, "uhhhhh..." And then she'd realize what was happening to her and she'd get all uptight and start fighting again... And, Charlie just sat over in the corner and sort of... "conducted the operation".

[INT. DAY – Prison S.L.O.]

JACK W: Nothing to do with it, hunh?

TEX: With God as my witness, I took no part in that poor girl's misfortune.

[INT. NIGHT – Ranch saloon]

> Again, the images of Simi's rape. This time showing Tex's involvement. Simi's SCREAMS carry over in echo to the next segment.

[INT. DAY – Prison C.I.W..]

PATTY: Simi? Ha, she didn't last too long. [Laughs] She was too hung up on what Mommy and Daddy taught her, her material needs and her ego. She couldn't survive, so she fled back to the establishment. That's okay, we didn't need her.

[INT. DAY – Prison S.L.O.]

JACK W: I'll say the name again...

TEX (agitated): Yeah, I remember her. [Pause] But as to what happened to her...

JACK W. (cutting Tex off): She was raped.

TEX: Yes, I know, but that was Charlie and Bobby. I had nothing to do with it.

[EXT. DAY – Los Angeles]

> Once out of viewing distance of the girls, Simi breaks into a sprint. She runs down an alley and turns a corner, falling against a garage to catch her breath. Haunted by sounds and images of her rape, she pulls the beads from her neck in a repulsed fury.

[INT. DAY – Prison C.I.W.]

JACK W: Did you ever hear from her again?

SADIE: No, she just vanished. I do pray for her now in my nightly prayers. [Pause] I just thank God that she got out when she did; otherwise she might well be in prison, too.

[INT. DAY – Basement of Mars' house]

> Dennis, Lucy, Mars and Stevie are still in the smoky basement, nude. Dennis is attaching a homemade silencer to the barrel of the .32 revolver with duct tape. The silencer is an empty 2 liter bottle, stuffed with wadded newspaper. On the television is Richard Kern's film, "You Killed Me First". Lung Leg is screaming out from the VCR.

LUNG LEG: Pray for me. You've got the nerve to pray for me. I'm just as... you're just as disgusting as I am! It's your fault! I've always hated you! You ruined me! You ruined my whole life! All my life...

[EXT. DAY – Cemetery]

> Sadie and Patty are posing next to tombstones for Tex, who is filming them with a movie camera. Sitting cross-legged on the grass nearby is Charlie, who is rolling joints. The PRESENT DAY Jack Wilson interview is heard over these visuals.

TEX (V.O.): Suddenly, there was a lot more talk about Fear and its usefulness. Be like an animal, be like a coyote. Use Fear to help you exist and to live in the Now.

[INT. DAY – Office/Linda interview '71]

LINDA: I think I tried to make myself believe I was a witch. I was Yanna, the good witch.

[INT. DAY – Prison C.I.W.]

SADIE: Charlie just shifted gears. We ignored the establishment and reality even more than we had before. We continued with the "Magical Mystery Tour".

JACK W: "Magical Mystery Tour"?

SADIE: Charlie got that from the Beatles. He called life, or the flow of life, "The Magical Mystery Tour". We were all one, one mind, one soul flowing within it and with it.

[INT. NIGHT – Documentary footage/Clem]

CLEM: It's a total state of paranoia... it's... man, when you're that aware, you can feel everything. You can see everything that moves, hear everything that makes a sound, you can smell every smell.. and when you're that aware.... you're at the Now.

[INT. DAY – Prison S.L.O.]

Clem, Patty.

TEX: This is when we started going out on "Creepy Crawl" missions.

[ANIMATION SEQUENCE: The screen suddenly bursts forth with psychedelic, kaleidoscope colors which change to colorful 1960's Pop Art-style cell animation of spiders and scorpions crawling about. The words "CREEPY CRAWL" flash on and off, in bright red and green letters, at the top and bottom of the frame]

[INT. DAY – Prison C.I.W.]

JACK W: Was it around this time that the Family started stealing to survive? Breaking and entering?

SADIE: We weren't breaking and entering. We creepy crawled those houses.

JACK W: You what?

SADIE (eyes lighting up): Creepy crawled them.

[EXT. NIGHT – An affluent neighborhood]

> A small group of Family members are standing outside the rear of a wealthy family's home. After silently slicing the window screen open with his buck knife, Tex carefully climbs

> through the window, followed by Sadie and Patty, who are carrying small sacks. Sunshine and BRUCE stand watch outside.
>
> The present day interview with Sadie continues in voice over during the creepy crawl segments.

SADIE (V.O.): It was basically cat burglary. Small groups of us would drive into the wealthy districts, pick a house and steal right from under the people's noses while they slept.

> In the dining room, Patty searches through the pockets of a sports jacket, draped over the back of a chair. Tex grabs a large silver tray off of a cabinet. In the bedroom, as a couple sleeps soundly, Sadie rises up from the floor and begins grabbing money and jewelry off of the dresser and placing it into her cloth sack. She snatches the couple's watches from their nightstand beside their sleeping heads.

NANCY (V.O.): You stay positive and confront your fears. You say yes to your fears, submit to them and overcome them. No sense makes sense. You can't get caught if you don't got thought in your head.

SADIE (V.O.): You had to be super aware at all times, you had to be sure of every move you made. Sometimes we'd drop acid before going out, to heighten our awareness level. We creepy crawled probably fifty houses or more and we were never caught, not once.

[INT. DAY – Prison S.L.O.]

TEX: Sometimes we would steal from the people's houses that we broke into, other times we'd just move the furniture around to freak them out when they woke up in the morning.

[INT. DAY – Prison C.I.W.]

SADIE (beaming): I was a master criminal.

[INT. DAY – Basement of Mars' house]

> As Lucy, Dennis, Mars and Stevie prepare for their mission, "You Killed Me First" continues blaring from the television. Stevie wraps the handles of two large butcher knives with red tape.

LUNG LEG (V.O.): I can't believe you've ever been alive. You don't deserve to live... I hate you... [GUNSHOTS] You gotta go too!

KAREN FINLEY: Elizabeth!!!

Lung Leg: "You Killed Me First".

LUNG LEG: My name is Cassandra. You killed me first! [GUNSHOT]

[EXT. NIGHT – Campfire outside of Ranch saloon]

> The Family is gathered around an empty chair at night, while a fire burns and drums are played. They all stare at the chair; listening to Charlie's grisly rap. Under the collective force of their LSD vision, the chair begins rocking.

TEX (V.O.): Charlie had this game, he'd gather us together around an empty chair... and we would take really strong LSD. All of us would stare at this chair while Charlie spoke. He called it the Fear Chair... He would tell us to imagine a rich, Establishment Pig sitting in the chair. "Suppose we just yanked his soft, rich ass out of his money-eating Cadillac and sat it right here. Now it's his trial..." We'd stare at this imaginary person and project his fear right back at him, keeping him immobilized. We'd fantasize that we might actually kill him with his projected fear... his own fear. Charlie would quietly mention things we could do to him... tying him up... gutting him like a pig... going to his home to steal all of his money, murder his family, chopping the bodies into bits, smearing eyeballs on walls... He made Bo and a couple other girls sick once, he was so graphic in his descriptions.......

[INT. DAY – Prison C.I.W.]

PATTY: Keep judging yourselves in Charlie, but don't look in the mirror!

[EXT. NIGHT – Campfire outside of Ranch saloon]

[TEX'S TRIP OUT/Fear Chair]

> Tex is mesmerized by the chair, the fire, the LSD and Charlie's sermon. He hallucinates seeing Kitty, nude, take a seat in the Fear Chair, holding a large mirror. His vision dives through the mirror, seeing the bloody future. This sequence is to be a homage to Roman Polanski's directorial rendering of Shakespeare's "MacBeth", Act 4, Scene 1, lines 125–140. We see Bobby, a bald Snake, Patty and The Husband, The Blonde Woman and Satan. Flash of the .22 Buntline revolver, behind a shattering mirror which reflects a burning pig's head.

TEX (V.O.): I don't remember exactly when my mind crossed over from reality to imagination... but there was no escaping it. Things seemed so doom-laden that summer... everything that Charlie said seemed to be absolute, divine/driven truth. And, Charlie wasn't preaching death of the ego any more... now he meant violent, physical death, when he said death is beautiful.. Death was beautiful, because it was what people feared the most. Death was merely an illusion anyway... because the infinite soul can never die.

[INT. NIGHT – Documentary footage/Gypsy]

GYPSY: If you're not dead, you will be, soon!

[INT. DAY – Basement of Mars' house]

> Dennis, Mars, Lucy and Stevie are still naked in the basement. Dennis' gun is outfitted with its crude silencer and Stevie has finished wrapping his butcher knife handles with red tape. Dennis chops out a line of cocaine on the bullet strewn mirror before him. As he snorts it, Stevie springs upright like a Jack in the Box and deftly twirls his knives. He is Johnny Twin Blade; The Crimson Avenger! He walks backward to Dennis' table and gazes at his pale reflection in the mirror. Suddenly, the mirror splits open to reveal fire and a glimpse of himself in the future, holding the knives, now covered with blood. Flash of burning newspaper with Jack Wilson's photograph. Fire.

[INT. DAY – Documentary footage/Sunshine]

SUNSHINE: Tex was in pretty bad shape. Charlie had told all of us to "cease to exist", but Tex never could. There was always some part of him fighting the whole thing, man. He wanted it both ways, you know? One minute he'd be bad mouthing Charlie and the next he'd be saying shit like, "I am Charlie and Charlie is me."

[INT. DAY – Prison S.L.O.]

TEX: It was too much. Too heavy. I felt I had to get back in touch with the person I was before I met Charlie. I hitchhiked to L.A. and called a girl I had known from Texas up...

JACK W: Rosina...

[EXT. DAY – Bus station/L.A.]

> Rosina pulls up to the curb and greets a very disheveled and scruffy looking Tex. Over these images, the Tex and Jack W. interview continues.

TEX (V.O.): Right. And when she picked me up... I suddenly felt embarrassed about how I looked, my dirty clothes and the fact that I had nothing, no money, no identity at all...

[INT. DAY – Prison S.L.O.]

TEX (continuing): I wanted back everything that I had worked so hard to get rid of while I was in the Family. I wanted to look sharp and have nice clothes and money. I wanted women who owned apartments and cars. Women with a little style, instead of the Hippy Girls who followed Charlie. Rosina took me under her wing and I was gone. I was renegade.

JACK W: Were you happy when you were away from the Family?

TEX: Yes, at first. I moved into Rosina's apartment and we became lovers. It was a very easy life.

[INT. DAY – Rosina's apartment/[EXT. DAY – Sunporch]

> A series of images follow each other, showing Tex and Rosina weighing out lids of marijuana, bagging them up, exchanging them for money with people, smoking bongs and lying on the sunporch in sunglasses, with mixed drinks in their hands. Tex's interview with Jack Wilson continues.

TEX (V.O.): Rosina made her income by dealing grass and LSD to her friends, nothing big, but enough to get by. When I combined my dope contacts with hers, we started making a lot of money. We sold lids for fifteen dollars, from kilos that cost us ninety-five dollars. I started buying nice clothes and record albums.

[INT. DAY – Prison S.L.O.]

TEX (continuing): I'd be sitting there, sucking down some water cooled Colombian Gold from a big bamboo water pipe and I'd think, "This is the life. Why in the Hell did I waste all that time out in the hills, taking orders from Charlie?"

JACK W: But you went back.....

> Tex clears his throat.

TEX: It was unnerving, I couldn't shake Charlie. Even though I thought I had rejected him, everything reminded me of him and his teachings. All of Rosina's friends, the people we sold to and partied with, all seemed to fit what Charlie had preached. I dropped acid one night at one of our many parties and it all came to a head.

[INT. NIGHT – Rosina's Apartment]

> A small party is in progress with many flashy, "Hollywood" phonies walking about, sipping champagne and snorting cocaine. Tex sits alone on the couch, bad tripping. To him, everyone at the party has on clown make-up and red bulb noses. Rosina walks up to him in clown make-up.

ROSINA: Are you all right?

> Tex simply stares at her in silence. Behind her, the guests are Rat People, Pig People and People Already Dead. Over these images is heard Tex's interview with Jack Wilson.

TEX (V.O.): It was all there for me to see. Charlie's gospel came right to the surface about how Establishment people were shallow and plastic, how much they were concerned with masks, self and money. About their willingness to rip you off. I felt ashamed for letting my ego come to life so quickly, for wanting material possessions.

[INT. DAY – Prison S.L.O.]

TEX: The next day I called the Ranch. Going back to Charlie seemed like the morally correct thing to do.

[INT. DAY – Prison C.I.W.]

JACK W: Tell me about Helter Skelter.

> Patty looks at him blankly.

PATTY: Helter Skelter is the name of a song, performed by the Beatles. [Pause] Period.

JACK W: But Charlie's Helter Skelter led to nine dead bodies.

PATTY: NINE dead bodies? What about the MILLIONS who are poisoned everyday by toxic wastes? When are people going to stop putting themselves before the air, the earth, the water, and the wildlife? People behave as if they can eat money and drink gasoline. What's going to be left for future generations?

[INT. DAY – Prison S.L.O.]

JACK W: So you ripped off a black dope dealer...

TEX: Yes, I did..... but he was never supposed to be in on it. I originally had just Rosina set up, but Lotsapoppa put his money in and came along.

[INT. DAY – Prison C.I.W.]

SADIE: Oh, the race war was something we believed in totally. It wasn't the reason for the murders, but the belief that there was going to be a great race war was something that hung in the atmosphere and drove us crazy.

[EXT. DAY – Driveway of house/Hollywood]

> An orange van, driven by Tex, pulls up to an ordinary looking house. Beside Tex is LOTSAPOPPA, a large, powerfully built black man, and Rosina. Tex shifts into park and turns the engine off.

TEX: Well, here we are. Give me the money.

LOTSAPOPPA: Why can't we come in and meet the man?

TEX: No. No. This guy is super paranoid, he's a speed freak. If I took you in there now, he would totally flip out.

LOTSAPOPPA: Well, you bring it out and I'll pay the dude...

TEX: No. No, man. No fronts. The man doesn't front to anybody.

LOTSAPOPPA: You'd be bringing it fifty yards from the house and running the money right back. That's not a fucking front.

TEX: I already told you...

LOTSAPOPPA: Besides, if I give you the money, now how do I know you're not buying bad product?

Lotsapoppa, Tex.

TEX: Look man, I know the difference between good dope and bullshit... Okay? [Pause] Look, he's a small time operator... he only deals with people he can trust, you know, like me. He's been in this business a long time.

LOTSAPOPPA: That's why I want to meet the man.

TEX: Hey look, he's not going to change his rules for me. Now do you want this or not? 'Cause I don't care, we can go right now.

> Lotsapoppa searches Tex's face for the trace of a lie.

TEX: C'mon Lotsapoppa. Give me the money. I'll be back in a flash.

> Lotsapoppa produces an envelope stuffed with cash.

LOTSAPOPPA: I don't like this.

> Tex snatches the envelope from Lotsapoppa and exits the van.

LOTSAPOPPA: Hurry up... I ain't got time to waste.

> Tex walks up to the house, turns and gives Lotsapoppa and Rosina the thumbs up signal. Lotsapoppa watches with narrowed eyes as Tex walks in the font door and closes it behind him.

Clarence, Rosina.

[INT. DAY – Dealer's house]

> Tex walks through the empty house and escapes out the back door with Lotsapoppa's money.

[EXT. DAY – Driveway to the house of the dealer]

> As Tex sprints into the thick of the neighborhood, Rosina and Lotsapoppa anxiously await his return. Lotsapoppa finally comes to the infuriating conclusion that he has been burned.

LOTSAPOPPA: Fuck!

[INT. DAY – A small room in Lotsapoppa's house.]

> Rosina is sitting on a ratty mattress, tied to a steam radiator. She is being guarded by CLARENCE, a friend of Lotsapoppa. Clarence is doing a line of cocaine on the table he is sitting at. A small rifle lies across his lap. After snorting, he becomes disoriented and turns to face Rosina.

CLARENCE: Don't look at me.

> There is a knock at the door. Rosina tenses up as Clarence, carrying the rifle, approaches the door. He leans against it softly.

CLARENCE: Who is it?

[INT. NIGHT – Prison S.Q.]

JACK W: Did Tex come back, after the burn, right away?

BOBBY: We didn't SEE or HEAR from his ass until a week later. He had lived it up and blown almost a thousand dollars. He tried to give the rest to Charlie when he came back, thinking nobody knew where it came from. Charlie was pissed off.

JACK W: Charlie shot Lotsapoppa...

BOBBY: Everybody knows that. Charlie was just being the father for the spoiled child, just the shepherd looking after his flock, dig? Right after Tex burned him, Lotsapoppa called the Ranch, madder than Hell. Charlie took the call. Lotsapoppa was screaming at him, "We're coming to that ranch to burn it down, unless you get us our money, motherfucker!" So Charlie cools him out and says, "Don't come here, I'll come over there. I'll be right over and we'll settle this."

[INT. DAY – A small room in Lotsapoppa's house.]

CLARENCE: Lotsapoppa isn't here. Come back when Lotsapoppa's here.

CHARLIE: Oh man, we drove a long way.

PATTY: Can we wait inside? Come on...

> Clarence gets tense.

CLARENCE: Shit. Fuck this. Fuck this.

> Clarence cautiously opens the door. Charlie and Patty enter the room. Charlie heads straight for Rosina.

CLARENCE: Where are you going?

> Patty rubs Clarence's chest in an effort to distract him.

PATTY: Hey baby, what's your name?

> Clarence throws her against the door.

CLARENCE: Get the fuck off of me!

> Clarence whirls back around, aiming his rifle at Charlie, who is on his knees beside Rosina.

CHARLIE: You poor child, you must be Rosina.

ROSINA: Yes.

CLARENCE: Hey man! I'm talking to you! Get over here!

> Charlie ignores Clarence.

CHARLIE: Marnie, would you untie this poor girl's hands?

> Patty obediently walks to Rosina.

CLARENCE: Where... Where're you going?! Look motherfucker, you keep her tied up! Where the Hell do you think you are?!

CHARLIE: Aw... Come on, man, this little woman couldn't out-muscle you. At least I wouldn't think so.

> Charlie laughs and Clarence comes charging at him with his rifle.

CLARENCE: All right motherfucker, get up! Get up! And put that fucking gun on the table!

CHARLIE: All right.

CLARENCE: Easy!

> Charlie removes the .22 Buntline revolver from the waist of his pants and holds it aloft.

CLARENCE: I said easy!

CHARLIE: It's going easy...

CLARENCE: Put it down!

CHARLIE: Nice and easy...

CLARENCE: Put it down.

> Charlie sets the revolver on the table.

CLARENCE: Where's this Tex motherfucker?

CHARLIE: I don't know, man.

CLARENCE: Where's our fucking money?!

[INT. DAY – Prison C.I.W.]

PATTY: Charlie thought Lotsapoppa was a Black Panther, Mr. Wilson...

[INT. NIGHT – A small room in Lotsapoppa's house.]

> Charlie is seated across from Lotsapoppa, at the table upon which is the .22 Buntline revolver lays. Patty is sitting with Rosina, while Clarence stands guard at the door, rifle in hand. The tension is high, all around.

CHARLIE: I feel that you're a reasonable person, open to reasonable conversation.

LOTSAPOPPA: I want my twenty four hundred dollars, little man. You got it?

CHARLIE: No, I don't got it, you know that. Nothing has changed since we talked on the phone, man. But I want to work this out, peacefully.

Charlie, Lotsapoppa.

LOTSAPOPPA (angry): Then why in the fuck did you come down here empty-handed? You're wasting my time. You better get your butt right out on that street and find Tex. Because if you don't, I'm going to hurt these girls. Badly. Very badly. And if Tex ain't got every last cent of that money, he's wasted. I'm gonna kill him. He's gonna be wiped out, you dig it?

CHARLIE: Hey, man, hold on. That's not necessary.

> Charlie picks up the .22 Buntline by its barrel. He offers the grip of the revolver to Lotsapoppa.

CHARLIE: Would you take this gun?

LOTSAPOPPA: I want my money...

CHARLIE: Take it as a gift from me, man.

LOTSAPOPPA (confused): A gift?

CHARLIE: Please.

> Lotsapoppa takes the gun from Charlie.

LOTSAPOPPA: Okay...

> Lotsapoppa shoves the barrel of the gun into Charlie's face.

LOTSAPOPPA: Okay.

> Charlie smiles, then rises from the table as Lotsapoppa keeps the gun aimed at him.

[EXT. DAY – Documentary footage/Sandra with Zezozoze.]

SANDRA: He's whatever a person wants to make of him. He's a mirror, actually... a reflection of yourself.

[INT. NIGHT – A small room in Lotsapoppa's house]

> Charlie is on his knees before Lotsapoppa, who has the revolver aimed at his throat. Patty, Rosina and Clarence watch, anxiously.

CHARLIE: Kill me. My life in exchange for my brother. Shoot me.

PATTY: Amen, Charlie.

> Lotsapoppa cocks the hammer back on the gun, but Charlie does not move. Lotsapoppa sighs and lays the revolver back on the table.

LOTSAPOPPA: Get up. Get up, dammit. I got no war with you. Just with the son-of-a-bitch that burnt me! Get up!

> Lotsapoppa grabs Charlie by the vest and jerks him to his feet.

LOTSAPOPPA: Marnie stays here with Rosina. [Pause] As insurance.

CHARLIE: Okay, brother...

> Lotsapoppa regards Charlie with curiosity, then decides to push him.

LOTSAPOPPA: They'll both be right here when you get back. If we don't fuck them to death.

> Lotsapoppa breaks into laughter, as does Clarence.

CHARLIE: I'll get Tex for you. Marnie, I'll be back soon, okay?

PATTY (scared): Charlie...

> Lotsapoppa's laughter subsides.

LOTSAPOPPA: Now you're making sense, little man.

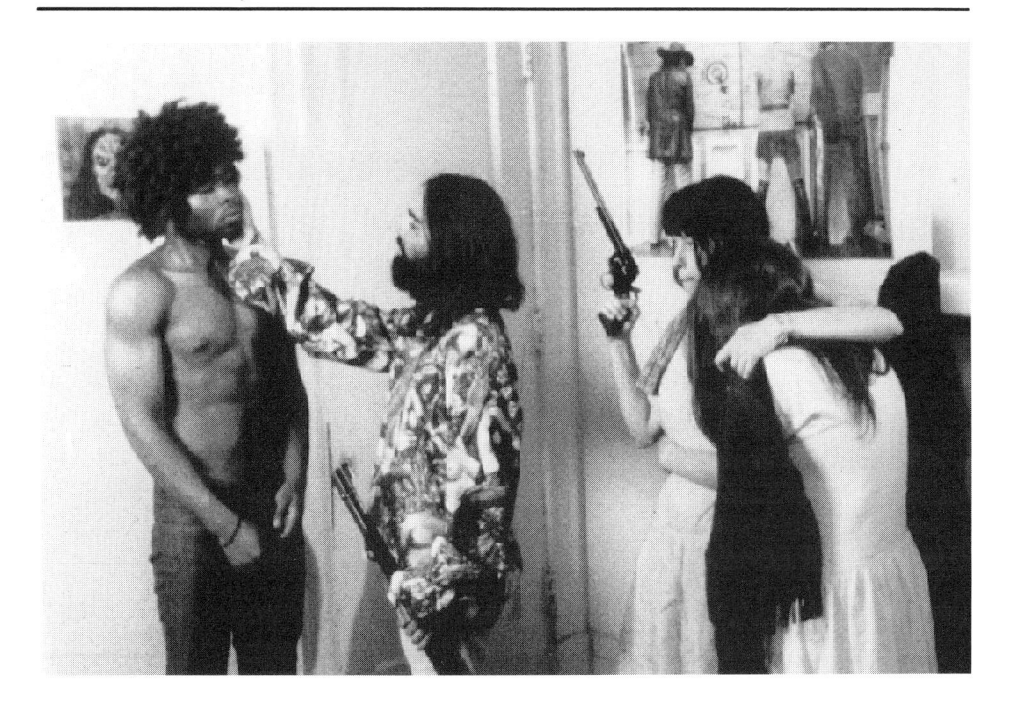

> Suddenly, Charlie grabs the revolver off of the table and points it at Lotsapoppa. Clarence immediately points his rifle at Charlie's head. Lotsapoppa stands up.

LOTSAPOPPA: What are you going to do, shoot me?

> Charlie squeezes the trigger and an empty CLICK is heard. There is a pause, then Lotsapoppa begins laughing again. Charlie relaxes.

CHARLIE: How can I shoot you with an empty gun?

> Charlie turns to Clarence.

CHARLIE: There are no bullets in it, man.

LOTSAPOPPA: All right you little fuck...

> Charlie aims the gun at Lotsapoppa again and fires. BLAM! The bullet hits Lotsapoppa in the chest, sending him reeling backward. He hits the wall and slides to the floor as Charlie turns the gun quickly on a surprised Clarence.

CHARLIE: Drop it!

Clarence puts the rifle on the floor with shaking hands. Patty and Rosina walk over to Charlie.

[INT. DAY – Prison Vacaville]

CHARLIE: I'm only as violent as I have to be. If I don't have to be violent, I'm not. But I was raised up to where if you didn't fight, you got fucked.

Charlie grins and laughs to himself.

[INT. DAY. – Prison C.I.W.]

SADIE: In everything that has been written, people overlook how much impact the shooting had on the future. The District Attorney dreamed up the lie that Charlie was trying to start a Black/White war that would become Armageddon. He wasn't trying to start it. It was already coming down as far as we were concerned. He was just reacting to it.

[FLASH CUT: A black and white reprinting of the Lotsapoppa shooting.]

[INT. DAY – Prison C.I.W.]

SADIE: Charlie was terrified that the Black Panthers would take revenge for Lotsapoppa.

JACK W. (interrupting): Who wasn't a Black Panther or even dead...

Sadie.

[INT. NIGHT – A small room in Lotsapoppa's house]

> Charlie has Clarence against the wall, at gunpoint. Beside Charlie stand Patty and Rosina. Charlie nudges the barrel of the gun against the collar of Clarence's shirt.

CHARLIE: That's a really nice shirt you're wearing there. I like it. I really do... can I have it?

[INT. DAY – Prison S.L.O.]

TEX: I remembered hearing about the cop who shot the sixteen-year old black kid a month earlier. I remembered the riots in Watts and the speeches by the Black Muslims in San Francisco. Martin Luther King Jr. had just been assassinated. So, Charlie's rap didn't seem far out at all. I felt that it was coming down, you know. Not next month, but right now, this month.

[INT. DAY – Jack Wilson's VPP suite]

> The image of Tex on the monitor freezes. Jack stares at his icy gaze.

JACK: You know that Lotsapoppa is alive today...

> Jack looks at Bob.

JACK: ...still carrying that .22 bullet lodged next to his spine. He was hospitalized for eight days, telling the police that he didn't know who shot him or why... During the trial the D.A. offered to arrange an operation for Bernard to remove that bullet and prove that it was fired from the same .22 Longhorn Buntline Special that Tex used... taking the bill off the City's titty.

>Bob looks at Jack blankly.

JACK: Obviously, Lotsapoppa turned them down... it was quite a risky operation.

>Bob is bored out of his mind. He searches for a reply.

BOB: If only Charlie knew then... What he knows now... one violent episode after another...

>Jack doesn't notice Bob's indifference.

JACK: That's right. For me, this is the real crux, the springboard for the killings that followed. It was the first domino to be tipped... setting off the others.

[EXT. DAY – Parking lot outside Jack Wilson's studio]

>Inside of a parked, beat up '79 Chevy sit Dennis, Mars, Stevie and Darren. They are smoking one hits of crack through a broken off television antenna. On their tape player jams Hardcore Metal. Mars finishes smoking her hit. Nobody seems to notice them.

MARS: It's gone, man. Here, pack him some more.

>Mars hands the metal stem to Dennis. He loads up another small rock.

DENNIS: You fucking guys geeking?

STEVIE: I ain't geeking on nothing, man.

MARS: I guess not. This shit fucking sucks. I can hardly geek off of it myself.

STEVIE: I like crack. It feels good and everything, but I don't need it or anything.

MARS: Well, who does?

STEVIE: You guys take too big of hits.

MARS: Jesus Christ! You fucking whine so much, man. Why don't you take your turn?

> Darren hands Stevie his one hit. Stevie snatches it up.

STEVIE: Thank you! Finally...

MARS: I thought I said it was fucking empty last time you handed it to me!

> Stevie lights up greedily.

[EXT. DAY – The horse corral at the Ranch]

> Clem and Patty are target practising with the Family's .22 Buntline revolver, while Bobby, Linda, Sunshine, Charlie, Sadie and her baby, Zezozoze, watch.
>
> Clem hands the revolver over to Patty.

CLEM: Now you try...

> Patty fires and misses.

CLEM: Squeeze the trigger. You're pulling.

> Sadie is softly tapping Zezozoze's nose with a flower. Zezozoze grabs the flower and begins eating it.

SADIE (laughs): Nooo. No, don't put it in your mouth. Stop it.

CLEM: Squeeze...

> Patty fires and misses again.

CLEM: You're pulling, not squeezing. Just do it easy.

> Shorty walks out of the old barn and strides toward the Family group with grim purpose.

SHORTY: I want to talk to you and your people, Charlie.

> Patty turns and shoves the Buntline revolver into Shorty's chest. Clem bursts out laughing as Shorty wrenches the gun from Patty's hands.

SHORTY: Never point a gun at anyone!

> Shorty turns and walks up to Charlie.

Clem, Patty.

SHORTY (angry): You tell me what happened to Simi.

CHARLIE: Simi who?

> Shorty looks up at Bobby, who is perched on the corral fence.

SHORTY: Where the Hell is she, Bobby?

> Bobby chuckles.

BOBBY: She got wise to what a bullshit life she had with you and George. We opened up her mind... and she split.

SHORTY: Her parents called. She hasn't been home for five days. You Goddamn Hippies better be straight with me.

> Bobby laughs at Shorty.

SADIE: We ate her up like a piece of Pumpkin Pie, and oh, was she sweet.

> Charlie withdraws his sword.

CHARLIE: Clem, Bobby. Get that gun away from him.

> Clem grabs Shorty's arm and they begin struggling for the revolver. Bobby hops down from the corral fence, runs up to Shorty and decks him with a right hook.

SHORTY: I'm going to have you all run in, on auto theft! I know how to handle you bastards!

CHARLIE: Better watch what you're saying, Shorty...

CLEM: Why don't you get out of here, you pig.

> Clem, Bobby, and Patty kick and spit on Shorty.

CHARLIE: Or I'm going to have your head in a box.

> Patty chases Shorty away.

PATTY: Oink! Oink!

SUNSHINE: Run, Shorty!

[INT. NIGHT – Documentary footage/Snake]

SNAKE: Snitches? Snitches will be taken care of.

[INT. TWILIGHT – Jack Wilson's VPP suite]

BOB: Well, Chief... it's six o'clock.

JACK: Already?

BOB: Yep, sure is, Annette's had the day off... I just might find two steaks on the grill and a bottle of cheap wine waiting for me when I get home.

JACK: Okay.... I'm going to stay here another hour or so, I think.

BOB: Okay... I'll be in about nine tomorrow.

JACK: Fair enough... have a good night. Say hi to Annette for me.

BOB: Sure... see you in the morning.

[EXT. TWILIGHT – Parking lot outside of Jack Wilson's Studio]

> Bob walks out to his nice, new car. He notices the four sitting in the battered '79 Chevy, parked three spaces away from him.

[INT. TWILIGHT – Beat up '79 Chevy]

> Dennis, Mars and Stevie watch Bob stoically. Satanic Black Metal is playing on the cassette deck at a loud volume. Mars gives Bob a peace sign.

[EXT. TWILIGHT – Parking lot outside of Jack Wilson's studio]

> Unlocking his door, Bob sees Mars giving him the peace sign. He gives a half-assed wave, then turns and quickly gets in his car and starts it.

> From a wide overview, the camera sees Bob's car pull out of the parking lot, leaving only the battered '79 Chevy and Jack Wilson's empty, parked car.

[INT. DAY – Prison S.L.O.]

TEX (sheepishly): I had to find out where I belonged...

[INT. DAY – Ranch house]

> Sunshine is in obvious haste. He is leaving as Tex walks in through the front door.

SUNSHINE: Tex, man! I gotta go, but I'll be back and we'll talk, okay?

> Sunshine turns around and yells.

SUNSHINE: Wake up you guys! Tex is back!

> Sunshine hugs Tex, then bolts out the door. Tex stands alone and hears stirring and voices in the next room. He glances down at a large glass fishbowl containing a few dollars and some change. A crude cardboard sign taped to it reads, "Donations for Helter Skelter". Tex wrinkles his brow at this. The door to the next room opens and Patty walks out, followed by a groggy Gypsy, Clem, and Cappy. Patty embraces Tex warmly. They kiss.

PATTY: I knew you'd come back.

CLEM: Hey brother...

GYPSY: Welcome back.

SADIE: Where the Hell have you been?

> Tex smiles and wipes a small tear from his eye. He gestures to the fishbowl.

TEX: What's this?

>Patty smiles.

PATTY: We've got a LOT to talk about.

>A THUNDERCLAP is heard as a storm rolls in.

[EXT. DAY – Field/the Ranch]

>Tex and Patty are making sweaty, savage love in the mud as a light rain sprinkles them. Tex climaxes and lays inert on top of Patty.

PATTY: Roll over.

[INT. DAY – Prison S.L.O.]

TEX: Things had changed in my absence from the Family. Charlie had discovered the Beatles' "White Album" and it had turned his head around. Along with the Book of Revelations in the King James version of the Bible, the White Album validated everything Charlie had been preaching while I was gone; that the Blacks would revolt and an all out race war would start. The end of the world, the Battle of Armageddon.

[EXT. DAY – Field/the Ranch]

> Tex is lying in post-coital bliss with Patty as the rain continues to sprinkle on them.

PATTY: Did you have any idea that you were one of the Apostles?

TEX: An Apostle? What the Hell is that supposed to mean?

PATTY: C'mon Tex. Why else would you and I be here right now? Why would any of us be here?

TEX: Charlie.

PATTY: That's right.

> Tex grabs Patty's hand.

TEX: C'mon Patty!

PATTY: Well, you know who he is, don't you? It's all true, Tex. I know about these things, I know it's all true. I used to teach Sunday School. I was studying to be a nun before I met Charlie.

> Tex sits up, shoving Patty aside.

TEX: The gospel according to Charlie is all you girls know.

PATTY: You're absolutely fucking right, Tex. Because Charlie is Christ and Christ is love and Charlie is love. That makes Charlie and Christ one. The Beatles laid it all out on the White Album. The four angels with the faces of men and hair of women? That's the Beatles. And the breastplates of fire? That's their electric guitars, see? And you know who the fifth angel is, don't you? Don't you?

TEX: I'm just so sick of this mind fucking bullshit.

PATTY: You better be ready…

[INT. DAY – Prison S.L.O.]

TEX: Charlie told us he could see "The Seal of God", the mark that protected some men from the plague of angels in Verse IV of the Book of Revelations, on our foreheads and could thereby tell who was loyal and who wasn't. He said that one third of mankind, wiped out in Verse XX for "the worship of idols of gold, silver, bronze, and stone", was the White Race and they would be destroyed in Helter Skelter for the worship of money, cars, and houses.

Patty: "It'll make Nazi Germany look like a picnic."

[EXT. DAY – Field/The Ranch]

Patty is preaching to Tex in the pouring rain.

PATTY: The time is going to come when all men will judge themselves before God. It'll be the worst Hell on Earth. It'll make Nazi Germany look like a picnic. And you've got to be ready for that, right now, right here, right now, just like that. And that's where we're at all the time.

[INT. DAY – Prison S.Q.]

BOBBY: All of the sudden, we weren't "coming from nowhere and going nowhere...", with "nothing to do but make love". Charlie knew what we had to do.

[INT. DAY – Prison C.I.W.]

SADIE: He never really gave orders, he was so evil. He'd just scare us to death with his preachings. Every night he would tell us that there was going to be a race war, and that Whitey and the Blacks were going to war and it was going to be the worst war that the world had ever seen. And he said that we had to be ready, to save the children, to rescue the homeless babies and carry them off to the desert for safety. And we had to start collecting dune buggies and guns, supplies and all these other things to help us survive. And then... he would just calmly pull out this buck knife and he said, "I don't know about the rest of you, but I'm gonna start carrying a knife."

[INT. DAY – Documentary footage/Clem]

CLEM: There's no good or no evil... there just is.

[INT. DAY – Prison C.I.W.]

SADIE (continuing): ...two weeks later, everybody is carrying a knife and Charlie is showing us the best way to slit a person's throat.

[EXT. DAY AND NIGHT – Buildings on the Ranch]

> A series of images follow as Sadie's interview continues in voice over. Tex, Clem and others are seen on the rooftops of the barns and ranch houses on guard patrol, with shotguns. This is followed by documentary footage of all the weapons (guns and knives) laid out on the wooden planks of the boardwalk, following the police raid. Several Family members lay on their stomachs in police custody, near the weapons. This is followed by black and white Police still photographs of the captured Family members and weapons pile.

[INT. DAY – Prison S.L.O.]

TEX: Charlie set up a twenty-four hour watch with armed guards and walkie talkies, all around the ranch. Everybody was super paranoid.

[INT. NIGHT – Prison S.Q.]

BOBBY: It was perfect timing because the Family was starting to drift apart on the surface. Now we had purpose. To save all the young love before it all came down. We'd still make music and orgy, but now it had this dark underbelly to it.

[INT. DAY – Prison C.I.W.]

SADIE: We lived in fear until we were arrested. What Charlie had foretold us with Helter Skelter suddenly seemed very real. It seemed to be happening. We had to survive by escaping to the desert. We had to finance our survival by any means possible.

[INT. NIGHT – Documentary footage/Clem interview]

CLEM: Just like there's no past and no future. Just now... that's all that's important.

[INT. NIGHT – Documentary footage/Squeaky]

SQUEAKY: We will kill anyone who gets in our way, PERIOD!

[EXT. DAY – Death Valley desert]

> Charlie and Sunshine are sitting alone in the desert, miles from the Ranch. Charlie's dune buggy sits silently off to one side. Both are sitting cross legged, Charlie has his sword and Sunshine is smoking a joint. It is blistering hot.

CHARLIE: Listen... listen to it speak. Now we have to listen because the city is gonna burn to the ground... out here, things aren't so crazy, you know. We can have our children and our children can teach us what we need to learn. Out here we're closer to the land and the spirit of life. It makes a lot of sense, you know.

SUNSHINE: L.A. is way too intense. It's doomsville.

> Charlie suddenly becomes distant.

CHARLIE: Sunshine... how long are you planning to stay with us?

SUNSHINE (caught off guard): Uhm... I wasn't planning on... [grins] ...I mean how would I leave? You gave away my car.

CHARLIE: What'd you mean I gave away your car?

SUNSHINE: My Plymouth Roadrunner, remember? You gave it to Randy when I first came to the Ranch.

CHARLIE: Whhooaa now. You gave it away. Can't give away what ain't mine.

SUNSHINE: You asked me what I could give to the Family.

CHARLIE: Right... I asked what you could give.

> There is a tension filled pause. Charlie stares straight at Sunshine, intimidating him.

SUNSHINE: [Pause] Do you want me to leave, Charlie?

CHARLIE: Now hold on... I didn't say nothing about leaving... I want you to be free.

SUNSHINE: I don't want to leave...

[INT. DAY – Office/Linda interview '71]

LINDA: Of course I loved Charlie. I felt like he was the Messiah come again.

[INT. NIGHT – Prison S.Q.]

Charlie as Christ.

BOBBY: Everything was Biblical and Apocalyptic. The Book of Revelations. We'd drop acid and role play the crucifixion of Jesus. Charlie loved it.

JACK W: It's been reported that you sacrificed animals.

BOBBY: [Pause] A few dogs. So what?

[EXT. NIGHT – An open field behind the Ranch]

> The Family, carrying torches and tripping in their Biblical finery, are moving out to a clearing while moaning a low mantra. Leading them as Jesus Christ is Charlie, wearing a grapevine crown and carrying the weight of a large wooden cross on his shoulder. Bobby is carrying a large black dog in his arms.
>
> As the Family moves into the clearing, they toss their torches into the pre-built bonfire pits, igniting them. Tex and Al strap Charlie to the cross and raise him up.

TEX: King of the Jews!

> As Clem feeds straw to the fire with shamanic fury, Bobby cuts the throat of the dog with a machete. Sadie sticks a glass goblet under the dog's neck and it quickly fills with blood. The Family disrobes as Charlie hangs on the cross.

[INT. NIGHT – Documentary footage/Clem]

CLEM: And the flames blew up like the Devil's breath!

[EXT. NIGHT – Open field behind the Ranch]

> Bobby sips the dog blood from the goblet and hands it to Sadie.

BOBBY: Drink from this, all of you, for this is my blood, the blood of the covenant, shed for many for the forgiveness of sins...

> Sadie drinks from the goblet and passes it to the others. All of the Family members sip from the goblet. The Family begins to become sexual with each other, bloody lips and tongues twisting. Charlie hangs on his cross, moaning. Sunshine, stoned on LSD, stares at Charlie. Sunshine is gasping for air.

SUNSHINE: I'm the Devil... I'm the Devil.. I'm the DEVIL!

CHARLIE: ...I'M THE DEVIL!!!!! [Laughs insanely]

[DISSOLVE]

The Family has taken Charlie from the cross and wrapped him in a Death Shroud. They are circling his inert body, chanting together... finding the collective mind, to will Charlie back to life.

THE FAMILY: RISE! RISE! RISE! RISE! RISE! RISE! RISE!

Charlie sits up, as the shroud slips off of him, alive! While the fires burn into the night, the Family members run about naked with their knives. They slice up invisible enemies, pretend to slice each other and yell and scream with Satanic abandon. Over these images Sadie's interview with Jack Wilson is heard.

SADIE (V.O.): Neither repented they of their murders, nor of their sorceries, nor of their fornication, nor of their thefts. And they had a King over them, which is the Angel of the Bottomless Pit.

[INT. DAY – Prison C.I.W.]

We see that Sadie is reading from the Bible.

SADIE (continuing): ....Whose name in the Hebrew tongue is Abaddon, but in the Latin tongue, hath his name is Exterminans.

Sadie closes the Bible and looks up.

[EXT. NIGHT – An open field behind the Ranch]

> As Patty makes love to Sadie, we see Charlie on top of Kitty. He begins laughing and transforms into a reflection of Satan.

[INT. NIGHT – Documentary footage/Kenneth]

KENNETH: I was starting to space it real bad... and I fucking looked over and Charlie looked like the Devil, man. I said, "Man, I think we're in Hell!" He said, "Yeah, ain't it groovy?"

[ANIMATION SEQUENCE: In a rapid succession of images, we see a tarantula crawling against a wall of flames, a snarling wolf's head and a scorpion, frantically clawing against a backdrop of an early morning sunrise]

[EXT. NIGHT – An open field behind the Ranch]

> As the fire burns, the Family is making love. Patty runs from group to group, splashing dog blood from the goblet on them. She finally joins Bobby and Sadie. The Family pumps and grinds to several climaxes.

[INT. DAY – Documentary footage/Sunshine]

SUNSHINE: I was flashing on some heavy weather ahead, if you know what I mean. I was getting some real weird pictures. So... I got out while the getting was good.

[INT. NIGHT – Loft in the Ranch house]

> Sunshine, carrying a lantern and a packed dufflebag, wakes Linda from a sound sleep.

SUNSHINE: I... I've decided to leave the Ranch tonight.

LINDA: What do you mean, leaving? You can't...

SUNSHINE: Look, will you go with me?

LINDA: Why? You can't leave. I overheard Tex and Sadie and they're watching you.

SUNSHINE: I've got to get out of here.

LINDA: Why? What is going on?

> Suddenly, Sadie peers through a wooden beam, spying on Sunshine and Linda.

SUNSHINE: I'm scared.

LINDA: What's wrong?

SADIE: What's in the bag, Sunshine?!

> Sunshine and Linda look up at Sadie, frightened.

SUNSHINE (nervous): Hi Sadie...

> Sadie begins laughing. Her laughter is echoed by Patty, who rises up from a trapdoor, wielding a large knife. She sticks it into the floor as she cackles.

PATTY: You can't kill kill...

[INT. NIGHT – Prison S.Q.]

BOBBY: A bunch of people with their backs against the wall, willing almost to...

JACK W: Kill somebody..

BOBBY: Oh yeah, in a split second. Kill crazy and throw your life away.

[INT. DAY – Prison S.L.O.]

TEX: Any traces of my own will or personality had totally dissolved by this time. I was just an extension of Charlie and I took my role as Enforcer very seriously.

[EXT. DAY – Death Valley]

> Tex stands on the seat of one of the Family's dune buggy fleet. He stands alone, parked in a remote area of the desert, wearing an expression of anger and impatience. Gypsy and BARBRA approach.

TEX: Where did you think you were going?

BARBRA: Look, what's the big deal? I just wanted to be by myself for a while!

> Gypsy holds up Barbra's eye glasses.

GYPSY: She was wearing these.

> Gypsy hands the glasses to Tex. Barbra snatches the glasses from Tex.

BARBRA: I like to see in focus!

GYPSY: You were running away!

TEX: Were you?

BARBRA: I wasn't running away! What is going on, all of the sudden? You're acting like the Ranch has become some sort of military camp!

TEX: Take them off.

GYPSY: Charlie told you not to wear them!

> Gypsy reaches for the glasses. Barbra defends herself.

BARBRA: But I want to wear them!

> Tex knocks Barbra's arms away, grabs her glasses off her face and snaps them in half. Dropping the fragments, he grabs a fistful of Barbra's shirt and pulls her close. Gypsy glares as Tex speaks in a deadly tone.

TEX: Don't you ever leave the ranch without telling someone where you're going! Next time, I'll kill you! We'll hang you up in a tree and cut your tongue out!

[INT. DAY – Office/Linda interview '71]

LINDA: Going out to Death Valley, you know, it made a lot of sense. Somewhere to raise our children and let them teach us the things we needed to learn. In a place closer to the land, the stars and the spirit of life.

[INT. NIGHT – Prison S.Q.]

BOBBY: You got no idea how desperate things were out there. I'm not talking frustration, I'm talking lunacy.

> Bobby stares at Jack W. in stony silence.

JACK W: Tell us about the man you were convicted of killing.

BOBBY: I have my own justice. I live by my own laws. I don't respect the laws of this society, because this society doesn't respect its own laws. I make my own laws and live by them.

JACK W: And what are your laws?

BOBBY: [Pause] I believe that what comes around, goes around. What goes up, comes down. That's how life flows and I flow with it.

[INT. NIGHT – Living room of GARY'S house]

> Gary is a Nichiren Shoshu Buddhist. He is chanting the final phase of his evening Gongyo, kneeling before his Butsudan.

GARY (chanting): Nam myo ho renge kyo. Nam myo ho renge kyo...

[INT. NIGHT – Prison S.Q.]

BOBBY: The whole thing with Gary was that he had burnt me on a thousand tabs of mescaline. I went there simply to get my money back...

[INT. NIGHT – Gary's living room]

> Bobby, Sadie and Gary are facing each other, kneeling on the floor before Gary's Butsudan. They are having a heated conversation.

GARY: He told me that he, "Wasn't responsible for the karma I was incurring". I told him I'd look after my own karma, thank you very much.

SADIE: Well, he didn't mean it that way. Did Charlie tell you the Panthers are coming down on us?

GARY: Look, I can see where this is going...

BOBBY: The Panthers have got nothing to do with it, all right? We're moving the Family out to the desert to create a new society. Now you can fit into that.

SADIE: Charlie found this hole in the desert. It leads to an underground river with a forest and trees...

GARY: Look, I'm sympathetic, okay? I've given you all use of my house... my cars. I've given you, given you all help in the times of need. But I'm not following Charlie into the desert. I have my life and it's here.

SADIE: We're not asking you to change, Gary. You can bring your... your...

> Sadie stumbles for the word.

GARY: Gohonza.

SADIE: Your gohonza out there. You can have everything there that you have here. We love you, Gary.

Bobby, Gary.

BOBBY: We need you, man.

SADIE: I need you.

GARY: No. All right? [Pause] You're still my brother and sister, but I must be true to myself.

SADIE: Last chance.

GARY: If there's any way I can help you...

BOBBY: It's going to take a lot of money for a move of this kind.

GARY: I'll give you forty dollars, okay?

BOBBY: How about twenty grand?

> Gary laughs.

GARY: How about it?

SADIE: We need that money, Gary!

GARY: What money, what are you talking about?

[INT. DAY – Prison C.I.W.

JACK W: How did Charlie know Gary?

SADIE: Music. Gary was a musician also. Actually a music teacher, I think. He was a very kind, gentle man.

JACK W: Why did he die?

SADIE: Charlie was convinced that Gary had inherited twenty thousand dollars. Charlie asked Gary to join the Family and move to the desert with us. Gary said no. [Pause] So Charlie sent me and Bobby to his house to convince him.

[INT. NIGHT – Gary's living room]

> Bobby, Sadie and Gary are facing each other, kneeling before Gary's Butsudan.

GARY: Where'd Charlie get the idea that I inherited anything?

> There is an uneasy silence.

BOBBY: Don't.... Don't. Don't do this. Man, you don't want me to do this.

GARY: You've both hurt me very deeply. I don't have a penny for you and I think you should leave right now.

SADIE: Bullshit.

> Bobby removes the .22 Buntline revolver from under his shirt and sticks it under Gary's nose.

BOBBY: We ain't kidding, Gary.

GARY: Bobby! What're you doing?

> Sadie stands up with Bobby, who keeps the barrel of the revolver pressed against Gary's face. Gary begins to panic.

GARY: Look, I don't know what Charlie told you, but I don't have twenty thousand dollars.

BOBBY (angrily): You're bullshitting me! Look man, just get the money and we won't hurt you. I promise.

GARY: Get out of my house right now!

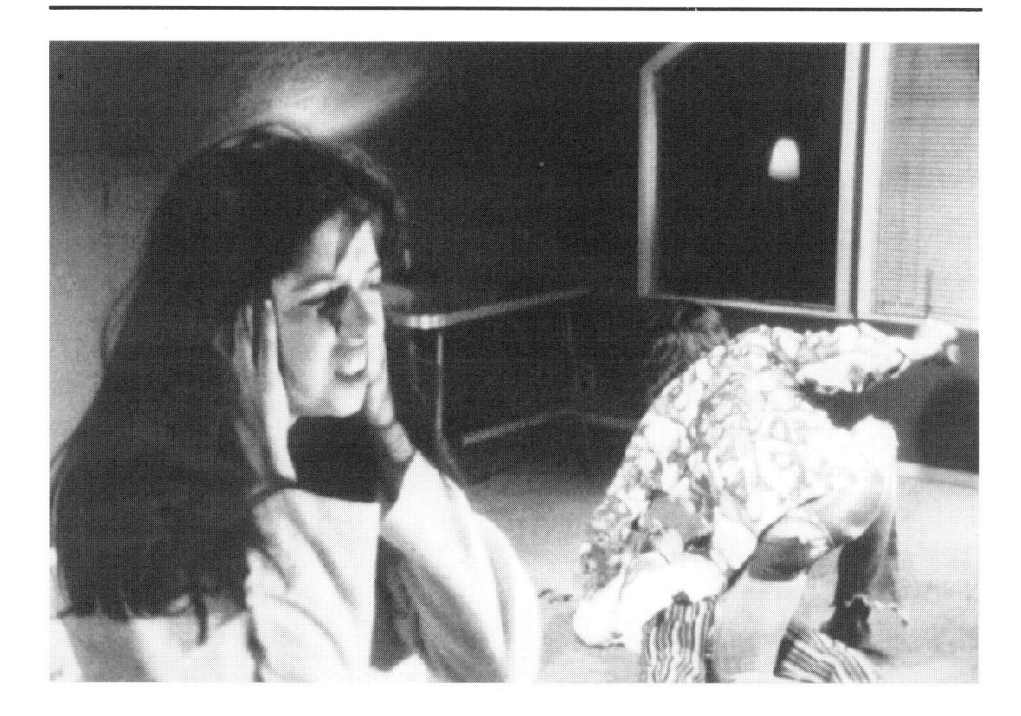

Bobby is silent, unsure of what to do. He hands the revolver to Sadie.

BOBBY: Watch him. I'm gonna find that money.

GARY: He's not going to find anything.

SADIE: Shut up!

[INT. NIGHT – Gary's bedroom]

Bobby is in Gary's bedroom. He is furiously searching under the mattress, under the bed and through Gary's dresser drawers.

[INT. NIGHT – Gary's living room]

Suddenly, Gary makes a jump for the revolver in Sadie's hand. They struggle and the gun fires, hitting a lamp beside the couch.

[INT. NIGHT – Gary's bedroom]

Bobby hears the gunshot, drops a strongbox that he had found and quickly runs out of the bedroom.

[INT. NIGHT – Gary's living room]

> Bobby runs into the living room, where Gary is trying to shake Sadie off of his back. Bobby grabs the revolver and strikes Gary with it several times until he falls, bloodied. Bobby pounces on top of Gary and grabs his head by the ears.

BOBBY: Tell me where that money is or I'll kill you.

> Gary begins chanting softly.

GARY (chanting): Nam myo ho renge kyo. Nam myo ho renge kyo.

BOBBY: Fuck!

> Bobby rises and walks over to Sadie, waving the revolver about wildly.

BOBBY (screaming): You stupid bitch! How did he get this gun?

SADIE (screaming): Don't yell at me, Bobby!

> Bobby runs Sadie up against the wall and grabs her jaw in his hand. He is deadly serious.

BOBBY: Look Sadie, we're not playing a game. If I give you a job, you do it, no excuses, understand?

SADIE: Let go of me.

> Bobby releases his grip and glances over at Gary, crumpled on the floor.

BOBBY: There's a strongbox in his bedroom. Get it.

SADIE (nervous): And bring it out here?

BOBBY: That's right.

> Sadie starts off to the bedroom. Bobby grabs her arm and yanks her back.

SADIE: What?!

BOBBY: You got any pills on you?

SADIE: Some bennies and seconals.

BOBBY: Give me a couple.

> Sadie pulls a plastic bag from her pants and fumbles for the pills.

BOBBY: C'mon, c'mon, c'mon!

> Gary moans weakly. Bobby runs to him and gives his face a savage kick.

BOBBY: Shut up!

> Bobby returns to Sadie, snatches two pills from her palm and swallows them. Sadie swallows a couple also as Bobby nudges her.

BOBBY: Get moving.

[INT. NIGHT – Gary's living room]

> Bobby is smashing the lock on the strongbox with a hammer. The lock gives. Bobby opens the box and finds only the pink slips to Gary's vehicles and some other documents.

[INT. DAY – Prison C.I.W.]

SADIE: Gary had no stomach for what was happening to him. He kept repeating that he had no money. He was tired and wanted to go to sleep. Bobby looked everywhere in that house for money.

JACK W: And you helped him...

SADIE: We had taken a lot of drugs. Bobby didn't know what to do.

JACK W: So he called Charlie?

> Sadie nods in agreement.

[INT. NIGHT – Gary's living room]

> Sadie is keeping the .22 Buntline revolver aimed at Gary's head. Gary is visibly beaten up. The living room is littered, following Bobby's search. Bobby is sitting on the couch, talking to Charlie on the phone.

BOBBY: We've trashed this place, we've turned it upside down. I don't know what else to... [Pause] Well, we got his... We've got the pink slips to his bus and his Fiat and we've got his mescaline. [Pause] I don't know if he has it.

Gary.

[Pause] All right, fine. Okay. [Pause] All right, fine. We'll be here.

>Bobby hangs up. Gary looks at him in disgust.

GARY: You're making terrible causes. Causes you'll pay for in later life.

BOBBY: Charlie's pissed at you, man!

GARY: You can't change the causes you have made, but you can counter them with positive ones.

SADIE: What the Hell?

GARY: You too, Sadie. Just go. Get out and you'll hear nothing from me, I promise you.

>Sadie stands up contemptuously.

SADIE: Tell that to Charlie.

>Sadie tosses the revolver into Bobby's lap, startling both Gary and Bobby. Bobby quickly aims the gun at Gary. Sadie walks across the room and switches on a small radio, sitting atop a table.

Bobby.

The radio blares forth with a popular tune and Sadie begins dancing to the beat. Bobby watches, incredulous. He walks to the radio while keeping an eye on Gary and switches it off. Sadie glares at him.

BOBBY: I can't think with that shit on.

Sadie indignantly strides back to the radio and switches it on. She resumes dancing. Gary watches them carefully for a chance to escape. Bobby sees through this and decides to let Sadie win her power play. He sits down on the couch, keeping the gun on Gary. Sadie hops and bops in front of Bobby. Bobby casually reaches for the bag of pills, grabs a few and swallows them.

BOBBY: Trippy chick... Yeah, yeah. Go ahead. Dance your stupid head off.

[INT. DAY – Prison Vacaville]

CHARLIE: I got the call from Bobby. Bobby's crying like some scared little girl. So I thought, "Gary's a freak behind this Japanese Buddhism, so I'll take my sword and impress him with a display of Oriental Swordsmanship." And that's all it was. Wasn't my fault he got cut.

JACK W: That's not what I heard, Charlie.

CHARLIE: See, now that's what you heard. There's a difference between what you heard and what is.

[INT. NIGHT – Gary's living room]

> Sadie is laying beside Gary on the floor, while Bobby remains on the couch. All are asleep. There are several loud KNOCKS on the door at the bottom of the stairs, waking the three.

BOBBY: That's Charlie, let him in.

> Sadie runs down the stairs to let Charlie in. Bobby walks over to Gary and pulls him up to his feet.

BOBBY: Get up. Get up!

> Charlie enters the living room with Sadie. He is carrying a large sword.

BOBBY: Hey Charlie. Where's Bruce?

> Charlie ignores Bobby. He glares intently at Gary's face.

GARY: Charlie... I... I don't think you know what you're doing by this.

CHARLIE: I want to talk about that money, Jack! Right now! Where is it?!

GARY: Take your people and get out.

> There is a silence as Gary and Charlie stare at each other. Suddenly, Charlie viciously whacks the left side of Gary's head with the sword, splitting his ear in half. The wound sprays Sadie with a shower of blood. Gary drops to his knees, screaming in agony. Charlie whirls around and sticks the point of the sword into Bobby's chest. He throws a coil of rope at Bobby.

BOBBY: Hey man...

CHARLIE: Don't.... come back without the money, man.

[INT. NIGHT – Prison S.Q.]

BOBBY: Charlie was never there, all right? During my trial, the prosecution wanted to involve Charlie in my case, which is difficult, because he was never there at any time. I cut Gary, when we were fighting... and it wasn't his ear, it was more like this little slash on his cheek.

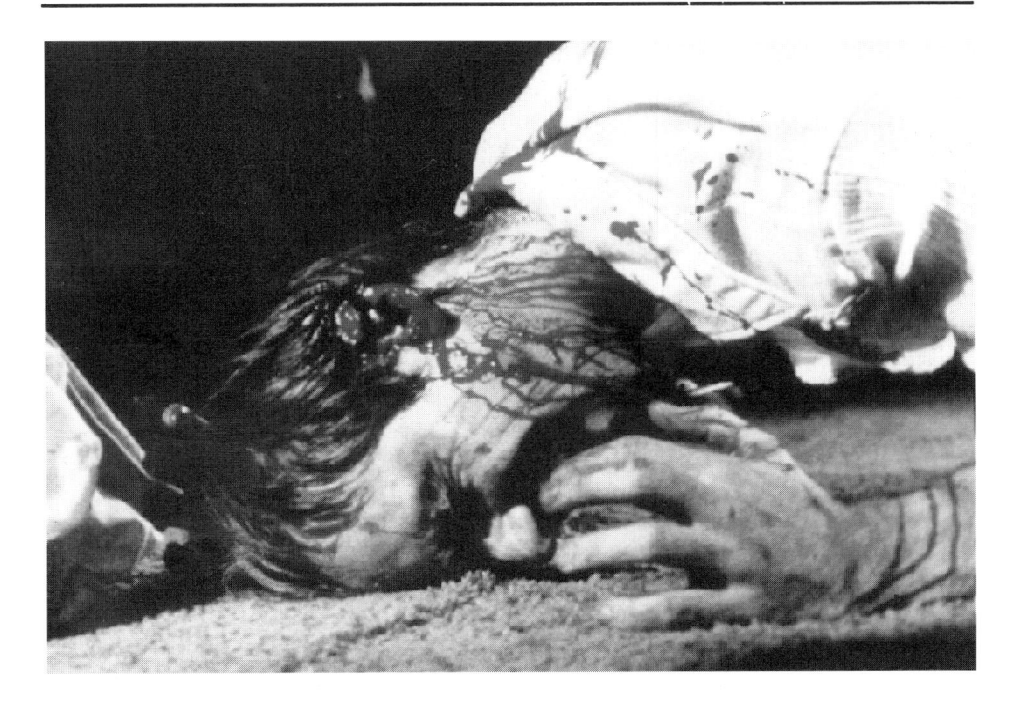

[INT. NIGHT – Gary's living room]

>Charlie turns away from Bobby and heads for the stairs. He stops by Sadie and gives her a shove.

CHARLIE: Clean up, woman.

>Sadie snaps out of her stupor and runs to the bathroom. Charlie leaves the house.

[INT. NIGHT – Gary's bathroom]

>Sadie washes the blood off of her hands and face and changes into a green vest that is hanging in the bathroom. She is shaken up.

SADIE (V.O.): I think Charlie knew what was going to happen, but we didn't. I know Bobby wasn't at all ready for what was happening.

[INT. NIGHT – Gary's living room]

>Bobby stands stupefied over Gary, who is moaning in great pain. Intense rage seizes Bobby. He throws the dagger to the floor and attacks Gary's Butsudan, ripping it from the wall and kicking the ceremonial ashes in the air.

Sadie.

[INT. NIGHT – Gary's bathroom]

> Sadie hears the crashings in the living room and heads out of the bathroom.

[INT. NIGHT – Gary's living room]

> Bobby is pacing back and forth over Gary's crumpled form when Sadie enters the room. She takes in the destruction and glares at Bobby.

SADIE: I'm gonna go get something to fix his ear.

> Bobby continues pacing.

BOBBY: You're not going anywhere.

SADIE: Look, we don't have any bandages and he is bleeding to death.

BOBBY (yelling): And he will keep bleeding until you tell us where that fucking money is, Gary!

SADIE: Shut up! He's in shock. He's not going to tell us a fucking thing unless we help him.

BOBBY: That's right. Fuck that!! I'm gonna rip this place apart and you're going to watch him. If Charlie says the money's here, it's here.

SADIE: I am going to get some medical supplies, right now!

> Sadie walks past Bobby.

BOBBY: You do what I say, Sadie!

SADIE: Fuck you!

> Bobby runs after Sadie and grabs her by the arm at the top of the stairs.

BOBBY: Wait a goddamn minute!

SADIE: What?!

BOBBY: Give me your pills!

> Sadie hands Bobby the plastic bag with disgust. Bobby takes several out and swallows them. He looks strung out.

BOBBY: You better come back, woman....

> Sadie turns and leaves. Bobby wipes the sweat from his brow and walks back to Gary. With unusual roughness, he ties Gary's hands together with the rope Charlie brought.

[INT. NIGHT – Gary's living room]

> Sadie has returned to Gary's house, after purchasing a sewing needle, dental floss, gauze bandages and a magnum of wine. Her and Bobby are drinking heavily as she sews Gary's ear back together with the dental floss. Gary is moaning softly with each pull of the needle and floss. Bobby chugs the wine left in his glass and glares at Sadie.

BOBBY: You're so fucking stupid.

> Sadie ignores him and lifts Gary's head up gently to her wine glass.

SADIE: Here Gary, drink this....

> Gary sips on the wine and coughs it up. The phone rings. Bobby ignores it. Sadie turns to him as it rings again.

SADIE: Would you answer that?

> Bobby shakes his head, "No". Sadie slams her wineglass on the floor and walks to the couch. She sits down and answers the phone, using a phoney sounding British accent.

SADIE: Hello? [Pause] Um...No, he's not here right now. [Pause] This is... This is Diane, a friend of Gary's [Pause] Um... He's in Colorado right now, visiting his parents. [Pause] Right. They were in an automobile accident. [Pause] I have no idea really. [Pause] Okay. [Pause] Okay. Will do. Thank you, goodbye.

> Sadie hangs up, feeling the panic rising in her. She rubs her face and approaches Bobby.

SADIE: Bobby... We've got to do something. We can't stay here much longer.

> Bobby stares at her.

BOBBY: We've turned this place upside down. What do you want to do?

SADIE: Well, call the Ranch. Ask Charlie...

BOBBY: Ask Charlie. Ask Charlie, sure. Charlie always has an answer, right? It's not always the right answer, but he always has an answer. What the Hell else have we ever done?

SADIE: That's right. What the Hell else have you ever done?

GARY: You bastards will fry for this.

> Sadie picks up Gary's prayer beads and tosses them at him.

SADIE: You're descending into the lower worlds, Gary. Where's your faith?

> Sadie kneels beside Bobby again. She refills his glass with wine and offers it to him.

SADIE: Call the Ranch, Bobby. Maybe Charlie will let us take him back there.

> Bobby takes the glass from Sadie and chugs the wine.

[INT. NIGHT – Prison S.Q.]

> Bobby looks introspective. He is smoking a cigarette.

BOBBY: I never meant to... [Pause] ...to hurt Gary. But one thing happened, then another. And then it all came down.

JACK W: And it was all good?

Bobby takes a drag off of his cigarette, and nods.

BOBBY: It was all good.

[INT. NIGHT – Gary's living room]

Gary is laying on the blood stained carpet, clutching his prayer beads and chanting weakly. Sadie is kneeling beside him, watching Bobby, who is on the phone with Charlie. Bobby is at wit's end.

BOBBY: Hey Charlie... no, nothing. Zero.

There is a pause in the conversation and Bobby visibly reacts to what he is told.

BOBBY: See you soon...

Bobby hangs up slowly and glares at Gary.

SADIE: What's going on?

Bobby picks up the dagger beside him. It glints sharply in the early morning sunlight. Gary realizes what is happening.

GARY: No..... no, Bobby. No.

Gary gets to his feet and runs for the stairs. Bobby jumps up from the couch and chases him, holding the dagger aloft.

GARY: Help! Help me! Help! Help!

Bobby grabs Gary's shoulder and spins him around. He stabs twice into the pericardial sac of Gary's heart. Gary stumbles down into the stairwell, dying. Sadie runs to Bobby, who stands holding the bloody dagger in a dazed stupor.

SADIE: Stab him again, Bobby!

Gary chants with the last breaths of his life.

GARY: Nam myo ho renge kyo. Nam myo ho renge kyo...

Sadie runs to the couch and pulls off a cushion.

SADIE: Got to do everything myself!

Gypsy.

    Sadie runs past Bobby and down the stairwell. She begins smothering Gary with the cushion as he fights for his life.

SADIE: Bobby, would you help me!

[INT. NIGHT – Prison S.Q.]

    Bobby stares coldly at the camera, smoking a cigarette.

[INT. NIGHT – Gary's living room]

    Bobby has joined Sadie in helping smother Gary. Gary struggles.

[INT. DAY – Prison C.I.W.]

    Sadie looks blankly at the camera, shifts her gaze to her lap.

[INT. NIGHT – Gary's living room]

    Gary is finally dead. Bobby and Sadie are both slightly splattered with his blood. They fall back against the walls, exhausted, then look blankly at each other.

[INT. NIGHT – Documentary footage/Gypsy interview]

> political piggy

GYPSY: To die is a beautiful thing. It's everything! It's every color in the spectrum of light, every sound... every note in all music!

[INT. NIGHT – S.Q.]

BOBBY: I returned and tried to cover my tracks... but I left some prints.

[INT. NIGHT – Gary's living room]

> Bobby, alone, is wiping down the radio, phone, etc., with a cloth. He covers Gary's fly-infested body with a green sheet. He wraps the cloth around his hand and holding his breath, dabs his finger in the pool of Gary's blood. Using the blood as ink, he writes "political piggie" on the wall in large crude letters. Next to it, he paints a panther's paw. This is followed by a black and white Police photo of the grisly message.

[INT. DAY – Prison C.I.W.]

JACK W: Why political piggie?

SADIE: To put it off on the Blacks. That's why Bobby made the paw print, you know. The Black Panthers.

JACK W: But it didn't work, did it? They arrested Bobby.

> Sadie is silent. She looks down at her lap.

[EXT. DAY – The horse corral/Ranch]

> Bobby is gazing at a large pile of horse shit that is abuzz with flies and bugs. He looks very depressed. Over this segment, the EARLY '70s interview with Sunshine is heard in voice over.

SUNSHINE (V.O.): After they snuffed Gary, everything at the Ranch was nuts. Charlie was preaching that to die is beautiful, that killing is the most beautiful thing in the world. Everything was death, death. Die, motherfucker, die! Death.

[INT. DAY – Documentary footage/Sunshine]

SUNSHINE: Everybody was looking at each other sideways and living in fear. There was no love any more.

INTERVIEWER: And that's when Bobby left the Ranch?

> Sunshine nods.

SUNSHINE: Right. I don't think he could take it. He was afraid that the cops were going to come to the Ranch, so he hopped in Gary's Fiat and took off. [Pause] And got busted.

INTERVIEWER: And you left shortly thereafter?

> Sunshine nods.

[INT. NIGHT – Prison S.Q.]

BOBBY: I had a lot of anxiety over getting busted. I split the Ranch on the pretence of ditching the car... One morning I was sleeping on the side of the road. In the car... some cops woke me up, called in the car... found the knife in the car... hauled my ass in. Effectively negating all of my creative efforts forever.

[INT. DAY – Inyo County Jail]

> Bobby, handcuffed, is thrown into a single cell. The two officers remove the handcuffs, then exit the cell quickly. They slam and lock the heavy door. Bobby leans to the slat in the door and screams.

BOBBY: It's all going to come down, you motherfuckers!!

[EXT. DAY – Outside of the horse stables/the Ranch]

> The Family watches as Charlie vents his rage on a stack of hay bales with his sword. Finally, he tires and flings his sword to the ground.

COUNTRY SUE: This is all your fault, Charlie!

SADIE: Shut up!

COUNTRY SUE: You killed Gary!

SADIE: You BITCH!

> Sadie attacks Country Sue. Charlie loses control.

CHARLIE (screaming): SHUT UP!

[INT. NIGHT – Documentary footage/black cyclorama/Nancy interview]

NANCY: As long as any of us is in jail, we're all in jail, you know? I'm walking around out here, but I'm in jail with every single young person that should be free. I'm in the Hall of Justice with Charlie and I'm on death row with Bobby.

[FLASH CUT]

[INT. NIGHT – Death Row]

    We see Bobby, dressed in his prison clothing, behind bars.

PATTY (V.O.): Wow, they got Bobby...

[EXT. DAY – Outside of horse stables/the Ranch]

    Charlie loses it and slaps Country Sue and Sadie around.

[INT. DAY – Prison C.I.W.]

LESLIE: This had nothing to do with the race war. No Blacks against Whites, no Armageddon, no Helter Skelter, no White Album! That wasn't what it was about!

[INT. NIGHT – Documentary footage/Nancy]

NANCY: So the girls got together to make up a plan to get Bobby out of jail. Charlie had nothing to do with it at all. Forget what the D.A. said, the motive for the murders was love of brother. We knew Charlie would give his life for brother.

[INT. DAY – Bobby's room at the Ranch]

    Leslie, Patty, Sadie and Linda are sitting in a tight circle.

SADIE: Are you sure he didn't mention me?

LINDA: All he said was that he was with a white girl.

SADIE: Oh, that's just great!

LINDA: He told them that when he and this girl showed up, Gary had already been knifed by some Blacks. So he and this girl helped Gary with first aid, as much as possible, you know, when you sewed his ear or whatever. And as a reward for helping him, Gary signed his cars over to Bobby.

PATTY: They believed that?

LINDA: No... I don't think so.

SADIE: We've got to get him out before he talks. He was freaking enough when it happened. We've got to get a lawyer.

PATTY: Lawyers cost money.

SADIE: How about a night of whoring? If all of us get dressed up and hit the streets, we could make a lot of money.

PATTY: I saw this movie once where the friends of this killer committed "copy cat" murders, in the same style that the guy had done. The cops let this guy go because they thought the killer was still at large.

LESLIE: That won't work.

SADIE: Yes it will! It will! Bobby wrote political piggie and made a paw print on the wall in Gary's blood. If we do it again, you know, write on the walls again, the pigs will be sure it's the Panthers, not Bobby. It'll be Helter Skelter!

[INT. DAY – Prison S.L.O.]

TEX: I'd dropped acid earlier that day and was asleep when Charlie came and woke me up. He asked me if I knew that Bobby had been arrested. I said, yeah, that's pretty rough. Charlie went on about how we were a family and we should never abandon one of our own. About how Bobby was our Brother and we were one.

> Tex clears his throat and drinks from the water glass.

TEX: He reminded me of the Lotsapoppa thing, how that had been my mess and he'd cleaned it up. How he had put his life on the line for me and had taken a life for me. Now, he said, it was time for me to pay my debt to him.

> Tex clears his throat again, looking uncomfortable.

TEX: He said the girls had a plan, but needed a man to pull it off. He told me to take the girls to Terry's old house, to kill whoever was there and take their money. "Make it a real nice murder, like a reverse Ku Klux Klan slaying," is what he said.

[EXT. NIGHT – Outside the saloon/the Ranch]

> Tex and Sadie are snorting speed, through a straw, from a Gerber's babyfood jar. The interview with Sadie continues in voice over through this segment.

[INT. DAY – Prison C.I.W.]

SADIE (V.O.): So before I knew it, I was dressed in my creepy crawl clothes and sneaking some speed with Tex, ready to go....

[INT. NIGHT – Loft in the Ranch house]

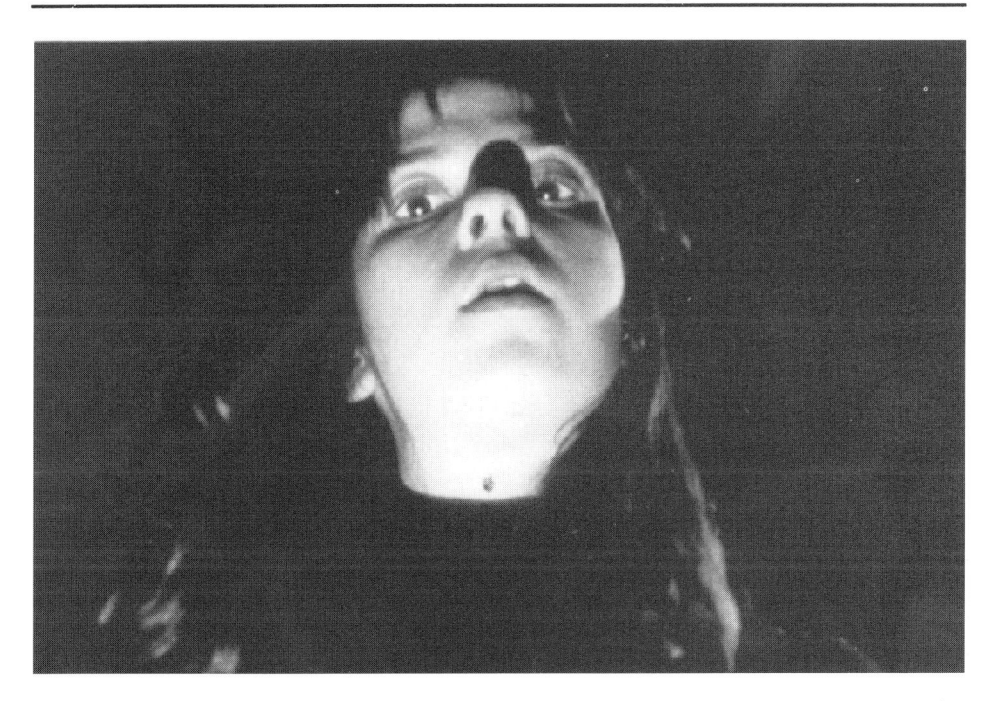

Sadie.

Linda.

Sadie, dressed in black, walks up to Linda, who is sleeping. Sadie shoves Linda's back with her foot.

SADIE: Wake up. Wake up!

Linda rolls over and looks up at Sadie.

SADIE: It's time, Linda. Now, you're going to need your driver's license, a change of clothes, put on dark clothes like I'm wearing and bring your knife.

[EXT. NIGHT – Main road to Ranch]

Linda, Tex, Patty and Sadie are sitting in a red '59 Ford, dressed in black. Charlie stands outside the car, leaning in the passenger's side window.

CHARLIE: Linda, I want you to go wherever Tex tells you. Everybody, do whatever Tex says. He knows what to do. And leave a sign. You girls know what I mean. Something witchy!

[INT. DAY – Prison S.L.O.]

TEX: So I led them there, I'd been there three times before.

[EXT. NIGHT – Highway]

> The '59 Ford is heading to Terry's old house on Cielo Drive. Inside the car, there is a great deal of tension.

TEX: Just don't worry about it. We're gonna get there.

PATTY: Oh fucking...

TEX: Just fucking don't worry about it.

LINDA: I'm sorry. Do you want to hear some music?

TEX: No.

SADIE: I wouldn't mind hearing some music.

TEX: Just shut the fuck up! Just shut the fuck up!

PATTY: Mellow out!

SADIE: I would step out of my casket like a freaky vampire and I would point at my victim... and I would dance in front of him...

TEX: Just fucking shut up!

PATTY: We'll calm down.

TEX: We're going!

LINDA: Okay... sorry!

TEX: Shut up!

SADIE: You're such an asshole.

PATTY: I wish you'd STOP!!

TEX: Shut up! Shut the fuck up! We're driving! GO!

> Tex stares ahead with hard, cold eyes.

[INT. DAY – Prison S.L.O.]

TEX: I had the girls wait in the car while I climbed the phone pole and cut the wires. We parked... ran down the embankment and climbed over a fence and barbed wire. We started toward the house and I saw a car coming down the driveway...

[EXT. NIGHT – Driveway]

As a YOUNG MAN drives his white, 1966 Nash Ambassador Sedan down the driveway, Tex turns to the girls.

TEX: Lay down!

Patty, Sadie and Linda crouch down on the edge of the driveway. Tex drops a large coil of white nylon rope from his shoulder and steps in front of the oncoming car, a buck knife in one hand and the .22 Buntline in the other. The car stops as Tex looms up to the driver's open side window.

YOUNG MAN: I won't say anything! Please!

The Young Man screams, raising his hands in defense of a stab from Tex's knife. The blade severs the boy's watchband and cuts deeply into his wrist. Tex raises the revolver to the boy's chest and fires. BANG! BANG! BANG! BANG! The Young Man slumps over in his seat.

[INT. DAY – Prison S.L.O.]

TEX: At first I was scared that somebody had heard the shots. I turned the engine off and rolled it back a few yards. I told Linda to keep watch... and I walked up to a window, slit open the screen and crawled in... I opened the front door and let Sadie in......

[INT. NIGHT – Living room]

In front of a fireplace, A LARGE MIDDLE AGED MAN is dozing on the couch draped with an American Flag. Tex, Sadie and Patty stand over him, weapons drawn. Tex turns to Sadie.

TEX: Go check for other people.

The Large Man slowly opens his eyes. He speaks with a Polish accent.

LARGE MAN: What time is it?

Tex kicks the man in the head. The man quickly sits upright, confused and angry.

LARGE MAN: Who are you?

Tex stands before the man, brandishing his knife and gun. The coil of rope is slung around his shoulder.

LARGE MAN: What do you want?

Sadie, Large Man, Tex.

    Tex stares at the man, his face locked into a grisly mask. He speaks with inflexible conviction.

TEX: I'm the Devil.... and I'm here to do the Devil's business.

    Tex steps toward the man. Patty realizes that she has left her knife back in the grass, outside.

PATTY: I don't have my knife!

    Patty runs out of the room to retrieve her knife as Tex drops the rope from his shoulder. He has his eyes locked on the man.

TEX: One more word and you are dead.

[EXT. NIGHT – Driveway]

    Patty runs to Linda, who is standing guard at the gate.

PATTY: Linda! I need your knife. Give me your knife!

    Linda, wearing an expression of shocked disbelief, gives Patty her knife.

PATTY: Listen for sounds!

[INT. DAY – Prison S.L.O.]

TEX: Sadie came back in, with this woman dressed in a nightgown and told me there was another couple in one of the bedrooms... I sent her back after them.

[INT. NIGHT – Living room]

> Tex is tying the Large Man's hands behind his back with one end of the nylon rope. Sadie leads a DARK HAIRED WOMAN into the room at knifepoint. The woman looks sadly over to the man. Patty enters the room from the hall.

SADIE: There's two more in a bedroom back there. A man and a woman.

TEX: Go get them. And bring a towel with you.

> Tex looks at Patty.

TEX: Watch her.

> Patty steps toward the Dark Haired Woman, knife at the ready.

[INT. NIGHT – Blonde Haired Woman's bedroom]

> A beautiful BLONDE HAIRED WOMAN, eight months pregnant and dressed only in a bra and panties, sits on the bed talking to a neatly dressed SHORT MAN. Suddenly, Sadie enters the room, flashing her buck knife.

SADIE: Don't ask any questions.

SHORT MAN: What do you think you're...

> Sadie presses her knife to the Blonde Woman's throat.

SADIE: DON'T talk! Come with me!

> The man and woman slowly stand. The woman grabs a blue negligee off of the bed and wraps it about her shoulders. Sadie marches them into the hall.

[INT. NIGHT – Living room]

Blonde Woman, Tex.

As Sadie marches her prisoners into the living room, the Blonde Woman freezes in her tracks. Sadie is carrying a towel.

SADIE: Move!

The Blonde Woman speaks in a quivering voice.

BLONDE WOMAN: I'm scared...

Tex steps up to the woman, grabs her arm and jerks her over to the fireplace.

SHORT MAN: Be careful with her, goddamn you!

Tex aims the revolver at the Short Man.

TEX: Silence! One more word and you will die.

LARGE MAN: He means it!

Tex grabs the Short Man by the shoulder and stands him next to both women. Tex looks at Sadie and motions towards the Large Man.

TEX: Tie his arms with that towel.

Short Man.

> Tex quickly ties the Short Man's hands behind his back with the nylon rope as Sadie ties the Large Man's arms with the towel. Patty watches, with wild eyes. Tex shoves the Short Man into a chair beside the fireplace, then loops the rope around his neck.

TEX: Don't move, don't speak.

[INT. DAY – Prison S.L.O.]

TEX: The methamphetamine crystal I had snorted earlier was blurring all of this together... time was telescoping... As soon as I had a thought, I was already experiencing the act itself, physically. To me, these people were not human... They were less than human... They were artificial.

[INT. NIGHT – Living room]

> Tex tosses the rope over a ceiling beam, it lands in a heap. He then picks up the coil of rope and loops it around the neck of the young Blonde Woman. As it tightens on her throat, she lets out a squeal of fear. Tex pulls the slack tight. She yelps again.

SHORT MAN: Let her go! Can't you see she's pregnant?!

Tex points the revolver at the Short Man's shoulder and fires.

The Short Man falls off of the chair, his weight on the rope jerking the Blonde Woman to her tip toes. She begins screaming. Tex steps toward the Short Man and kicks him in the face. The Dark Haired Woman is straining to remain calm while the Large Man on the couch is, unknown to the others, working his hands loose of the rope.

DARK HAIRED WOMAN: Please! We'll give you anything you want...

TEX: I want all of the money you have here.

DARK HAIRED WOMAN: I have money in my room. Please, let me get it for you.

    Tex looks at Sadie.

TEX: Go with her.

    Sadie, with knife extended, walks the Dark Haired Woman out of the room. The Blonde Woman is quietly crying. Tex and Patty look at each other and then at their prisoners. The Short

Man, laying in his own blood, lets out a moan. A large haematoma is swelling up on his left eye.

[DISSOLVE]

[INT. NIGHT – Living room]

Sadie marches the Dark Haired Woman back into the living room. Tex grabs her by the arm and stands her beside the Blonde Woman.

TEX: How much do you have?

Tex loops the rope around the Dark Haired Woman's neck as Sadie counts the money. He motions to Patty.

TEX: Take the rope.

Patty steps forward and takes hold of the dangling white rope. She pulls it taught, forcing the women up on their tip toes with the Short Man acting as dead weight.

SADIE: Seventy-two dollars.

Tex is enraged. He screams at his captives.

TEX: Seventy-two dollars! Is that all you've got?!!

DARK HAIRED WOMAN: How much do you want?

TEX: I want thousands!!!

The Blonde Woman tries to compose herself.

BLONDE WOMAN: That's all that's here, but we can get more if you'll give us time...

TEX: You know I'm not kidding...

BLONDE WOMAN (quietly): I know.

Tex looks at the Large Man, then at Sadie. Tex flips off the hall light switch with his elbow, then walks over to a table beside the couch and kicks a lamp off of it, sending the room into semi-darkness. The Short Man groans again and tries to move forward on his elbows. Tex steps over to him and kneels beside his crumpled form. The women burst into hysterical screaming as Tex stabs the Short Man repeatedly.

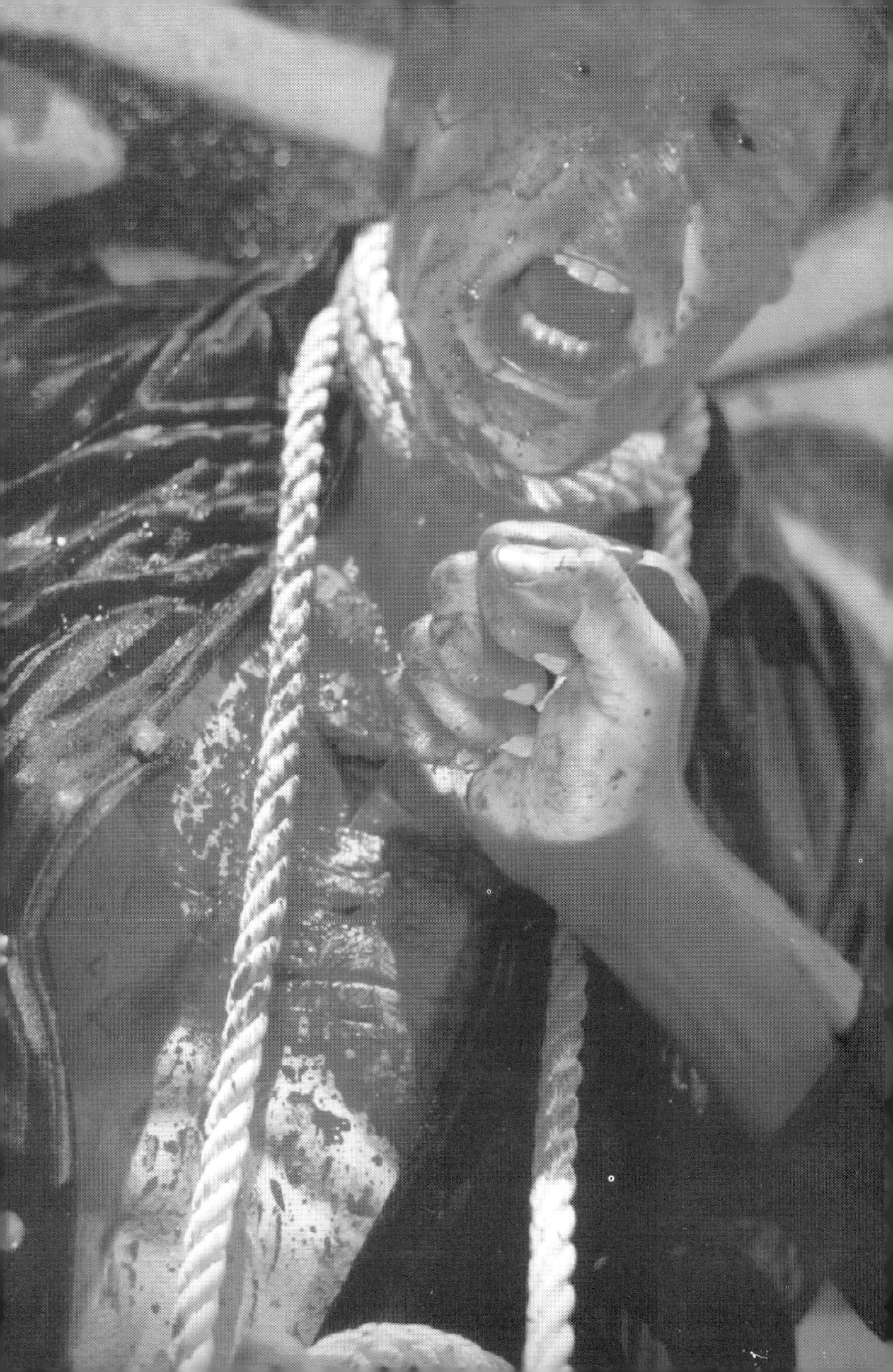

DARK HAIRED WOMAN: Please! Oh, God, please! Please!

TEX: I'm the Devil!

> Patty pulls tighter on the rope, choking the women. Sadie walks over to the Large Man on the couch.

DARK HAIRED WOMAN: What are you going to do with us?!

TEX: You are all going to die.

> A despairing moan rises up from the captives. Tex looks at Sadie and motions toward the Large Man, who is struggling to free himself. Tex becomes a reflection of Satan.

TEX: Kill him!

> The Large Man breaks free of the rope and towel as Sadie sticks her knife in his ribs. He grabs Sadie by her hair and they tumble onto the couch. Sadie blindly stabs behind her, striking the man's crotch and legs, as he beats her with one fist and pulls her hair out with the other. He stands and runs to the front door with Sadie hanging onto his back, her knife lost in the fight. Tex runs up to the man and stabs him as he opens

the door. Sadie falls to the floor as Tex and the Large Man spill out the door onto the front porch.

[EXT. NIGHT – Front porch]

Tex fires the revolver point blank into the Large Man's left axilla and front right thigh. He pulls the trigger again, but the gun misfires. The man, enormously powerful, continues fighting for his life.

[INT. NIGHT – Living room]

Sadie runs to the couch desperately searching for her knife. The Dark Haired woman frees herself from her noose and runs into the hall. Patty drops the rope and chases her. The Blonde Woman stands in shock.

[EXT. NIGHT – Front porch]

Again and again, Tex beats the Large Man's skull with the handle of the revolver, smashing half of the grip into pieces. The man lies still. Tex jumps up and races into the house, his black turtleneck sweater bloody and his eyes shiny.

[INT. NIGHT – Kitchen]

Patty has the Dark Haired Woman trapped against a kitchen counter. The woman's hands are cut and bleeding from protecting herself. Tex runs up to her and she lowers her arms.

DARK HAIRED WOMAN: I give up.... take me.

Tex slashes the Dark Haired Woman's throat with his knife and beats her head with the revolver's broken grip. Patty stabs her repeatedly in the lungs and abdomen. The woman collapses to the floor.

[EXT. NIGHT – Front porch]

Linda has walked to the house from the gate. She sees the Large Man, covered with cuts and his own blood, staggering toward her.

LARGE MAN: God! Please help me!

Linda is frozen with guilty fear.

LINDA: I'm so sorry!

As the Large Man limps out onto the front lawn, Sadie appears, knifeless, at the front door.

SADIE: Give me your knife, Linda!

LINDA: Make it stop! Make it stop!

SADIE: It's too late!

LARGE MAN: Help! Police! Somebody, help! Help!

SADIE: Tex! Tex! Tex!

Tex sprints out of the front door to the Large Man, tackling him on the grass. Tex stabs until the man is silent and still. Tex stands, dripping blood and walks to the house.

[INT. NIGHT – Living room]

Tex walks quickly through the front door into the room. Patty and Sadie sit with the Blonde Woman on the couch, the rope still looped around her neck. She is blubbering, tears streaming down her cheeks.

BLONDE WOMAN: Please... please. I don't want to die. Please!

[EXT. NIGHT – Back porch]

With her blood turning her white nightgown red, the Dark Haired Woman slowly opens the glass double doors and steps out onto the grass. She walks silently across the moonlit lawn, looking like a supernatural apparition. She stops and quietly falls to the ground, dead.

[INT. NIGHT – Living room]

On the couch, Sadie has the Blonde Woman's arms pinned behind her back. Tex and Patty gaze at the convulsing woman, their knives at the ready.

BLONDE WOMAN: Take me with you and let me have my baby! I want to have my baby! I want to have my baby!

SADIE: Look bitch, I don't give a shit about you, I don't care if you're going to have a baby. You'd better be ready 'cause you're going to die and I don't feel a thing about it.

PATTY: Kill her!

The Blonde Woman screams as Tex stabs her left breast. He stabs her again and Patty joins him. Sadie lets the girl fall to the floor where Tex and Patty continue to stab her. Finally, there is an immense, all consuming quiet. Sadie whispers to the others.

SADIE: Are they all dead?

TEX: I'm going to make sure.

> Tex stands. Patty stands.

PATTY: I'm going to find Linda.

> They start for the front door. Tex turns back to Sadie.

TEX: Remember to write something. Something that will shock the world!

> As Tex and Patty exit the room, Sadie dips a towel in the pool of blood on the Blonde Woman's chest.

NANCY (V.O.): You have to have a real love in your heart to do this for people...

[EXT. NIGHT – Front porch]

> While Tex runs from the corpse of the Large Man to the body of the Dark Haired Woman, stabbing them repeatedly, Sadie spells "pig" on the front door with the bloody towel. This is followed by a black and white Police photo of the grisly message.

Tex, Prison S.L.O.

[INT. NIGHT – Documentary footage/Squeaky]

SQUEAKY: What's the big deal? A million babies are born and die each day.

[INT. DAY – Prison S.L.O.]

TEX: Charlie was waiting for us when we got back, sitting naked in the moonlight. He asked if we had any remorse for what we had done and of course, the right answer was "no".

[INT. NIGHT – Documentary footage/Snake]

SNAKE: I remember Patty telling me about it and then I went through a change and I thought, "Right-on... I guess we did it."

[INT. DAY – Prison S.L.O.]

TEX: The next night, Charlie gathered Sadie, Clem, Leslie, Patty and me to go with him. Linda drove, of course, since she had the only valid driver's license. Charlie took us to this house where he used to party and said that we were going to do the one to the right of that house. He said that last night had been too messy and we were going to do this one differently. So, he went in

Wife, Patty.

and tied up the couple that lived there with some leather laces and he came back out and told Patty, Leslie and me to go in and kill them. But not scare them. Don't tell them that we're going to kill them, so they don't get scared and put up a fight...

[INT. NIGHT – Living room]

> Patty, Tex and Leslie are inside of an upper class home, holding a middle aged, Italian couple prisoner. Tex holds the husband on the couch at bayonet point, while Leslie and Patty march the wife out of the room.

WIFE: Please stop it! Please!

HUSBAND: Where are you taking her? She's my wife!

TEX: Shut up!

[INT. NIGHT – Bedroom]

> Tex and Patty have the Wife at knifepoint in the bedroom. Her hands are tied behind her back, as are her husband's, who is held at knifepoint by Leslie in the living room. Tex takes the pillowcases off of the pillows on the bed.

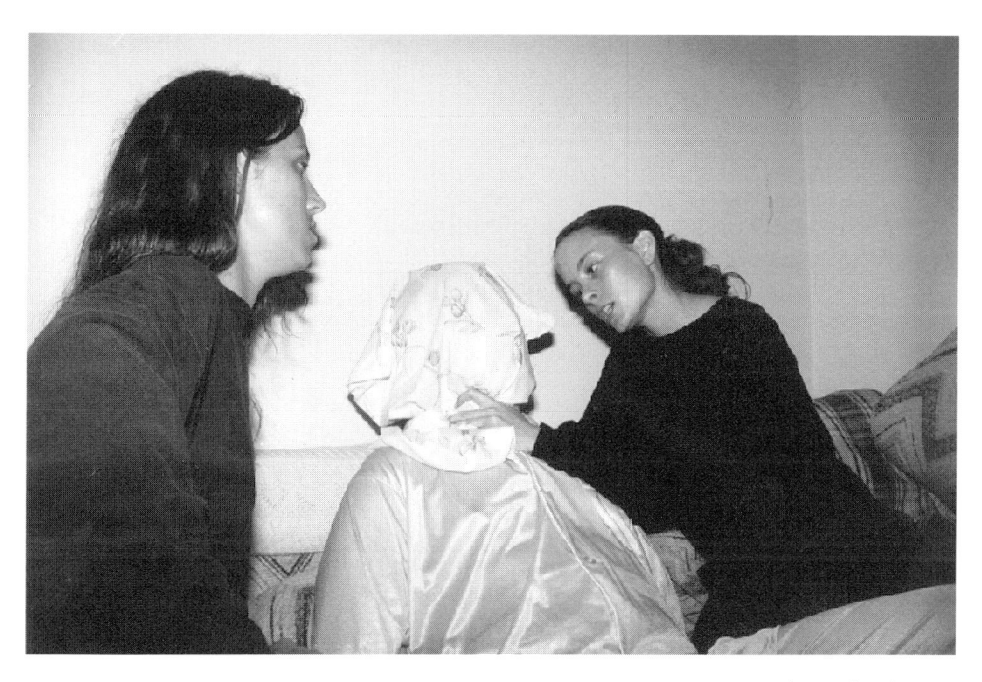

Leslie, Husband, Patty.

TEX: Unplug that lamp!

> Patty unplugs the lamp cord as Tex pulls the empty pillowcase over the Wife's head.

WIFE: Please, I want to be with my husband!

HUSBAND: What are you doing to my wife? I'll give you anything you want!

> Tex gives Patty a pillowcase for the Husband as he begins wrapping the lamp cord around the Wife's pillowcase-covered head.

TEX: Shut him up!

> Patty exits the bedroom and enters the living room from the hall, approaching Leslie and the Husband with the pillowcase. His eyes fill with panic.

HUSBAND: You're going to kill us, aren't you?!

[EXT. NIGHT – Front of house/Linda in car]

> Linda is quietly freaking out in the car while listening to the screams. She turns to the off-screen driver, past Clem.

LINDA: Let's go, Charlie... please.

The car moves out of the frame.

[INT. NIGHT – Kitchen]

In the kitchen, Leslie is searching through the kitchen drawers, excitedly looking for a weapon. In the next room, the Husband is screaming for his life.

HUSBAND (O.S.): Please! Don't kill me! Nooo...!

[INT. NIGHT – Living room]

Tex is holding the lamp, whose cord is bound tightly around the Husband's pillowcase covered head. Tex begins stabbing him with a large bayonet. The Husband shrills horribly.

[INT. NIGHT – Bedroom]

In the bedroom, the wife begins shrieking from inside her pillowcase. She stands up.

WIFE: What are you doing to my husband?!

[INT. NIGHT – Prison C.I.W.]

LESLIE: Charlie made sure that I went that night. He kind of made me feel guilty... he said that I should want to do it, because it was going to help Bobby.. and I was.. I was in love with Bobby.

[INT. NIGHT – Bedroom]

Patty, holding a buck knife, stands up with the Wife as Leslie enters the bedroom, carrying a carving fork and a steak knife. As the Husband's screams continue from the living room, the Wife begins screaming and twirling violently in a circle. The lamp, extending from the cord wrapped around her pillowcase covered head, begins swinging in a broad arc, keeping Patty and Leslie at bay.

WIFE (hysterical): Help! Murder! Help! Leno!

PATTY: Tex!!! Tex!

Tex runs in through the door with his bloody bayonet extended. He advances and is clobbered on the side of the head by the swinging lamp. Patty uses her buck knife. Patty stabs the Wife several times in the back, chasing her down onto the floor to finish the job. Leslie stands, horrified. Tex runs out to finish the Husband.

[INT. NIGHT – Bedroom]

Tex is smoking. He sits with Patty and Leslie, next to the Wife's corpse. He looks at Leslie.

TEX: Did you kill her?

LESLIE: No.... Patty did.

TEX: Well, you gotta stab....

Tex gets up and walks to the Wife's corpse. He lifts up her nightgown, exposing her bare buttocks. He sits down as Leslie stands, clutching the fork and knife.

TEX: Stab.....

As Tex watches and Patty laughs, Leslie begins stabbing the lower back and buttocks of the Wife's corpse.

[INT. DAY – Hall of Justice]

Newsreel footage of Patty being escorted to Court by Police Officers. The media and onlookers swarm around her.

PATTY (V.O.): If you are willing to be killed, you must be willing to kill... you gotta stab.

[INT. NIGHT – Living room]

Patty and Leslie stand over a dazed Tex. He sits beside the corpse of the Husband. Tex's eyes have changed color. The girls laugh. Patty drives the steak knife into the dead Husband's neck. Leslie starts giggling, again, and plunges the fork into the dead Husband's abdomen. It wobbles back and forth as Leslie laughs satanically.

[INT. NIGHT – Prison C.I.W.]

LESLIE: I know now... that what I did... was to Leno and Rosemary... and not things..., and NOT pigs. God, I'm so sorry. I just want to get out of here, so I can make something good with my life.

She breaks into honest tears.

[INT. DAY – Prison S.L.O.]

TEX: I had Patty write on the walls and refrigerator with their blood. The girls ate some food while I took a shower, then we hitch hiked back to the Ranch.

> The word "Rise", written on the wall in blood, flashes onscreen, followed by the words, "Death to Pigs", also written on the wall in blood. "Healter Skelter", written in blood on a refrigerator, flashes onscreen, followed by a black and white still photograph of same. The word "War", carved on the dead Husband's stomach, is flashed onscreen and replaced by a black and white Police photo of the same. A wider black and white photograph shows the Husband's full corpse. Then a final wide black and white photograph of the Wife's corpse in the bedroom.

[INT. NIGHT – Documentary footage/Nancy]

NANCY: They're willing to be in jail. They know that they're in jail for everybody. Maybe we'll all have to go to jail before we can get them out. Maybe we'll have to go up to the jail and say, "Hi, take me." But they know they're facing the gas chamber and they don't care. That's what people don't understand... they don't care... and they're willing to die, so that all young people can be set free.

[INT. NIGHT – Documentary footage/Clem]

> Clem sits, holding a rifle.

CLEM: Snitches will be taken care of.....

[INT. DAY – Documentary footage/Sunshine]

SUNSHINE: Charlie said they had to kill Shorty. He had to have Clem chop his head off.

INTERVIEWER: Did you see this?

SUNSHINE: This happened after I left... But I heard that Shorty wouldn't die unless they chopped his head off. They kept stabbing him, but he wouldn't die. He kept saying, "Why, Steve, why?" Steve, that's Clem's real name. So Charlie told Clem to chop his head off. Clem took a machete and cut his head off and it rolled into the mud, bloop... bloop... bloop.

[EXT. NIGHT – Campfire/the Ranch]

> An animated tale is being spun by Leslie, Patty, Nancy, Gypsy and Sandy to two "Straight Satan" motorcyclists as Clem looks

on. Clem is wearing Shorty's hat. The idea here is that the dialogue should come fast and furious, one line overlapping the next as the girls strive to one-up each other in their effort to scare the bikers.

GYPSY: Sadie was shooting her mouth off about the piggies we bagged on Cielo...

PATTY: Charlie said he knew too much...

SANDY (giggling): He punched her out...

BIKER 1: Shorty?

SANDY: Charlie.

LESLIE: So we cut him to ribbons...

BIKER 2: Shorty?

GYPSY: Right.

NANCY: First we dosed him...

LESLIE: We hog tied him while he was tripping...

PATTY: We stuck needles under his fingernails...

SANDY: And in his eyes...

LESLIE: Through his nipples...

PATTY: And cock...

SUSAN: And balls...

GYPSY: He pissed himself.

SANDY: Piss and blood...

LESLIE: Then we drug him through the mud...

GYPSY: He was screaming for his life...

SANDY: Charlie gave the word...

LESLIE: And we stabbed him like Caesar...

PATTY: Everybody, the whole Family...

[EXT. DAY – The horse corral/the Ranch]

> The Family is standing over Shorty, who lies in the mud, beaten and tied up with horse harnesses. Charlie spits on him as the Family waits, knives out and ready.

CHARLIE: It's not nice to snitch, Shorty....

> The Family tears into Shorty, stabbing him hundreds of times.

[EXT. NIGHT – Campfire/the Ranch]

SANDY: But he wouldn't die, we just kept...

SUSAN: Stabbing and stabbing.....

GYPSY: So Clem cut his head off...

LESLIE: We cut him into nine pieces...

PATTY: And buried him in nine places...

SANDY: His legs are buried right under you.

> The girls laugh ghoulishly. The Bikers, for all of their outward indifference, are genuinely spooked.

[INT. DAY – Prison S.L.O.]

TEX: Well... the girls made up that story about us chopping him up into nine pieces. Even the prosecutor put that in his book... But when Clem led the police to the skeleton, they found it intact, of course.

[INT. TWILIGHT – '63 Biscayne car]

> Tex is wrestling with Shorty in the back seat. Shorty has been abducted and beaten severely. They are driving out to the desert. Tex yells at Charlie, who is driving. Clem rides in the passenger's seat, the .22 Buntline revolver at the ready.

TEX: Pull over!

SHORTY: Please God, Nooo! NOOOO! NO!!!

[EXT. TWILIGHT – Desert outside of the Ranch]

Squeaky and Gypsy.

Shorty is out of the car as soon as it hits its brakes. Tex jumps out after him and tugs on the rope circling Shorty's neck. Shorty falls to his knees. Charlie gives the order and Clem jumps from the car. He places the tip of the barrel of the gun against Shorty's forehead. He shoots, blowing Shorty's brains onto the front, right headlight of the Biscayne.

[INT. NIGHT – Documentary footage/Gypsy and Squeaky]

GYPSY: The Revolution is ready and as soon as Charlie gets out, it's on, the Revolution is on! If you try to hurt Charlie... You'll all die!

SQUEAKY: I knew it was all perfect.

GYPSY: Sure... as perfection is.

SQUEAKY: I had a brother once, who went to war, it's the same love, and got shot and got killed...

    Squeaky snaps her fingers.

SQUEAKY (continuing): ...just like that. For NOTHING! It's the same thing, exactly. Love is being killed everyday. Every single day love is being killed.

[INT. DAY – The Hall of Justice]

> In a fast montage, we see newsreel footage of Sadie, Patty and Leslie walking through reporters and flashbulbs, on their way to a formal hearing. The last shot is of Tex, turning through the strain of movie lights, to deliver a crushing look of hatred at the camera filming him, as he enters court.

TEX (V.O.): We're all in this together... you gotta stab!

[INT. NIGHT – Prison C.I.W.]

PATTY (bitterly): As long as Charlie is locked away in his asylum/prison/ grave, you can say anything you want about him. Anything. You can lie in more movies and bogus books for money. You can pretend to play like him, joke about his suffering, and draw your very life from his blood. But you have not the soul to face him.

JACK W: Anything else?

PATTY: No.

[INT. NIGHT – The Hall of Justice]

> Sandy, outfitted in a hooded blue robe, is speaking to a multitude of reporters, cameras and microphones.

SANDY: You're a lot of vultures. You are. You live off the sacrifice of the young people. You're bloodsuckers... you are... with your little phallic symbols, you know? Excuse me...

[EXT. DAY – Street corner of Temple & Broadway]

> Members of the Family keep a vigil on the street corner, handing out flyers.

SNAKE: We're waiting for our father to be set free.

AL: Kill your parents!

NANCY: You don't realize...

> The whole group screams out one.

SIDEWALK VIGIL: It's the second coming of Christ!!! Judgment Day is coming, people!!!

[FLASH CUT: INT. DAY – Holding cell]

> Leslie is getting her head shaved.

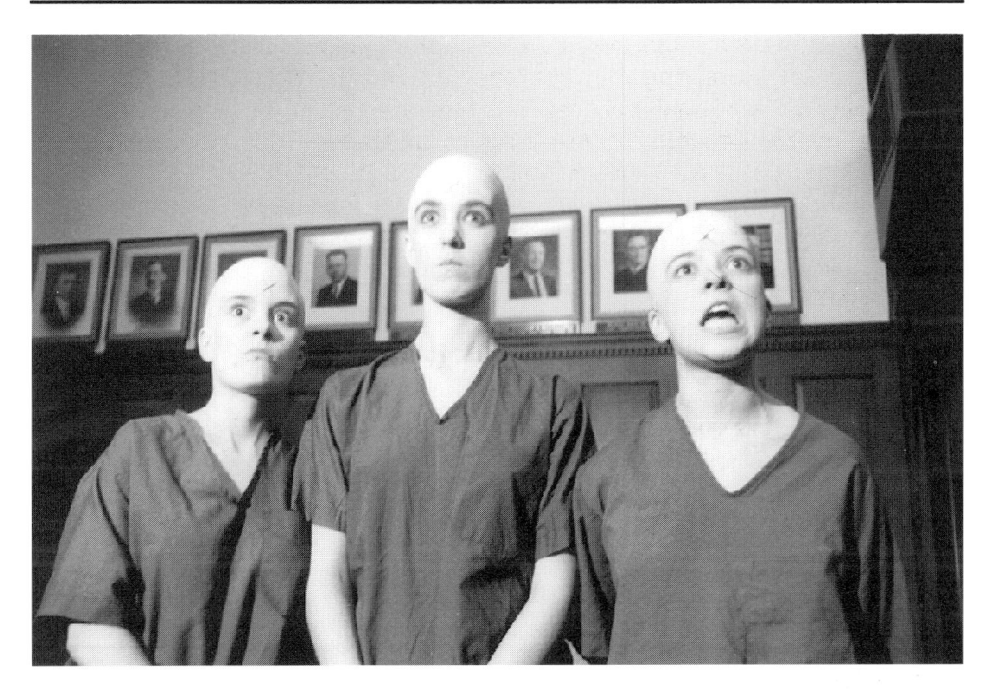

Patty, Leslie, Sadie.

[INT. NIGHT – Documentary footage/Snake]

SNAKE: Leslie's attorney? Ronald? [Begins laughing] Yeah... the press called him, "Leslie's Hippy Lawyer"... We thought he was cool... but he was just like the others... he was the first of the retaliation murders...

[EXT. DAY – Bench on Temple & Broadway]

> We quickly see some newsreel outtakes of Ronald, having a cigarette.

[EXT. DAY – Sespe Creek]

> Horrifying newsreel footage of Ronald's badly decomposed body, lying in between boulders. Long dead.

[EXT. DAY – Street Corner of Temple & Broadway]

> The Charlie Vigil is vocal and angry for the Reporters.

SNAKE: We are all facing the gas chamber!

KENNETH: Hey man, hey man, what do you think would happen, if one night seventy-five heads were cut off?

Jack Wilson, Dennis.

[INT. DAY – The Hall of Justice]

> Patty, Leslie, Sadie and Charlie have been declared guilty. The women stand, bald and defiant.

PATTY: You've just judged yourselves!!

SADIE: You better lock your doors and watch your own children!

LESLIE: Your whole system's a game, you blind stupid people, your children will turn against you!!!

[INT. DAY – The Hall of Justice]

> Newsreel footage of the three bald women walking downstairs, through reporters and cameras.

[EXT. DAY – Corner of Broadway & Temple]

SNAKE: DEATH! That's what you are all gonna get!!

[EXT. NIGHT – Parking lot outside of Jack Wilson's studio]

> Dennis, Mars, Stevie and Darren gather, outside of the door to the studio. They are ready to strike. Dennis grabs a tire iron

from Mars. He holds it tight. In his head, he hears the recordings of Jim Jones.

REV. JIM JONES: I will fight! I will fight! I will fight! I will fight! AAAHHHHHOOOWWWHHHHAAAAAHHHHOOOOOOWWWAAA!!! Let the night roar with it! Let the night roar with it! AAAHHHHHOOO-WWWHHHHAAAAAHHHHOOOOOOWWWAAA!!! Because they can hear us! They know we mean it! AAAAWWWAAHHHHHOOOOOWWWEEEE!!!

[INT. NIGHT – Jack Wilson's VPP suite]

SANDY: Your children will rise up... and kill you.

> Jack freezes the image. He reaches into his shirt pocket and removes a pack of cigarettes. He puts one between his lips and flicks a lighter. Just as he lights the tip, the calm is shattered by the sound of the front door window being smashed. Jack hears the unlocking of the door latches and rises to his feet. Suddenly, through the entrance to the editing suite, in walks Mars, Darren, Dennis and Stevie. Mars is carrying a towel, Stevie has two large kitchen knives and Dennis is holding a handgun, whose barrel is duct-taped to a 2 liter plastic bottle, stuffed full of newspaper. Jack is astounded. Darren is taping it all with a VHS videotape camera...

JACK: Wait a minute!

MARS: ...These children who come at you with knives, they're your children! You taught them, I didn't teach them... I just tried to help them stand up!

> Before Jack can make a move, Dennis aims his gun at Jack. The bottom of the newspaper-filled, plastic bottle bumps Jack's forehead. Dennis squeezes the trigger, blowing a hole in Jack's head. The powder burn ignites the newspaper inside of Dennis' home-made silencer. Before Jack's body can hit the floor, Mars wraps her towel quickly around his head, guiding Jack to the carpet. Dennis extinguishes the fire by stamping on the plastic bottle with his boots. Stevie straddles Jack's chest and stabs his heart repeatedly, to stop the flow of blood. On one of the television monitors in the studio, static and snow blare forth; it is on this screen that we see "CHARLIE'S FAMILY" spelled in Jack's blood by Mars, using her towel. Stevie begins slicing his shirt off with his butcher knives. Dennis laughs at him. Stevie drops his knives and screams at the ceiling.

[DISSOLVE]

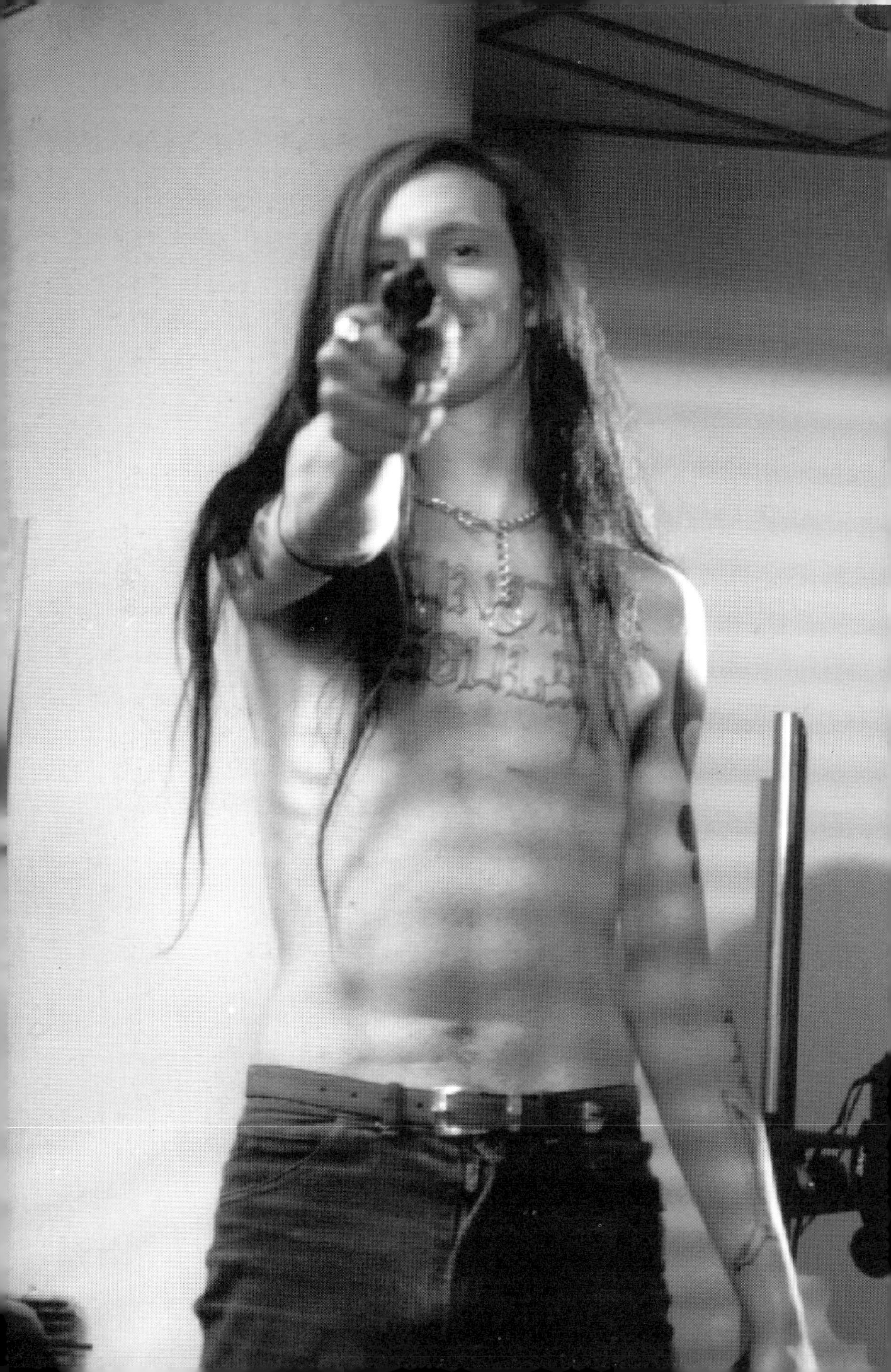

TATE CONT.

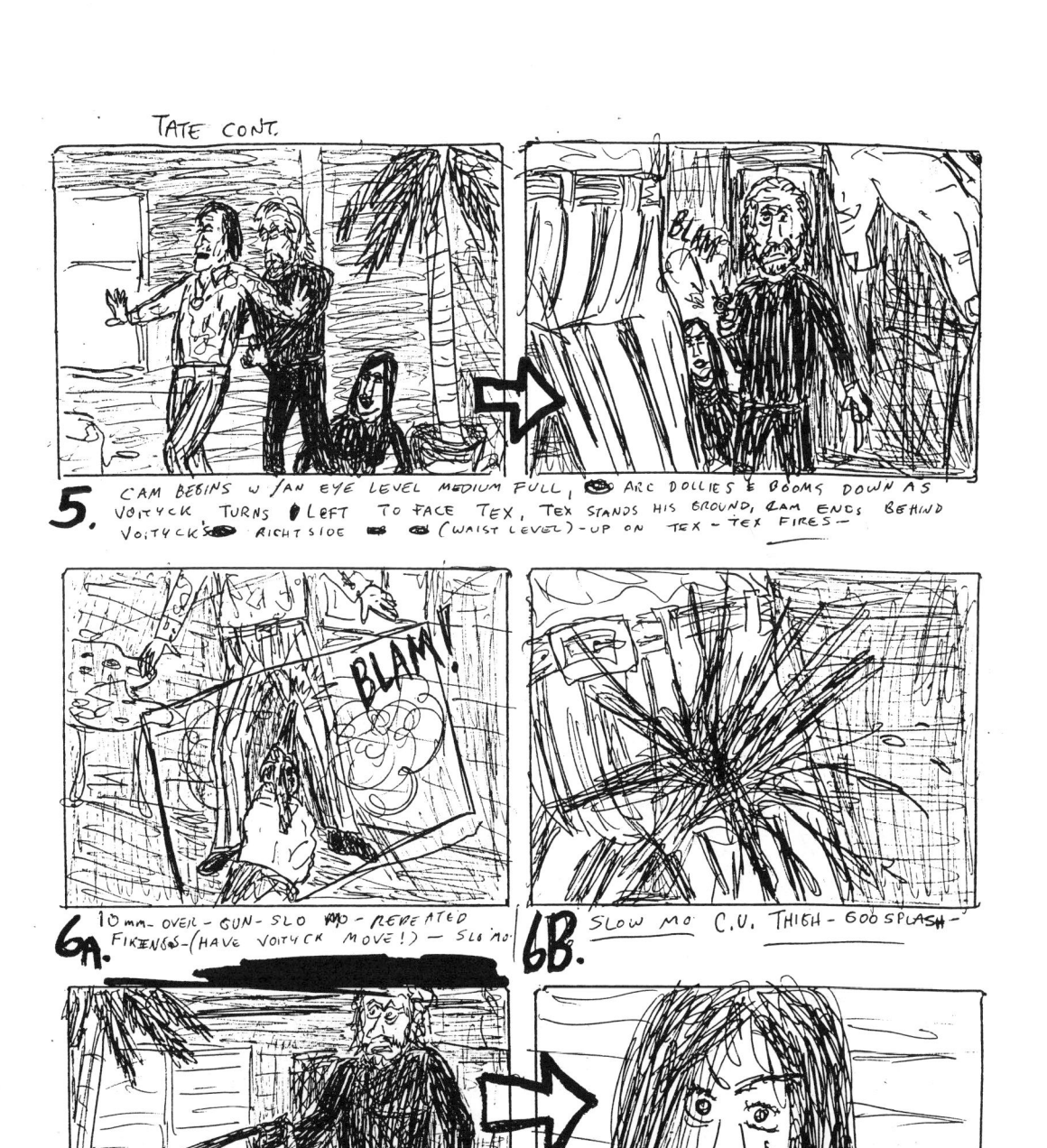

5. CAM BEGINS W/AN EYE LEVEL MEDIUM FULL, ARC DOLLIES & BOOMS DOWN AS VOITYCK TURNS LEFT TO FACE TEX, TEX STANDS HIS GROUND, CAM ENDS BEHIND VOITYCK'S RIGHT SIDE (WAIST LEVEL) - UP ON TEX - TEX FIRES -

6A. 10mm - OVER - GUN - SLO MO - REPEATED FIRINGS - (HAVE VOITYCK MOVE!) - SLO MO

6B. SLOW MO C.U. THIGH - GOO SPLASH -

7. CAM LOW - SHOOTING UP AT TEX, .22 EXTENDED - HE MISFIRES - CAM DOLLIES FOREWARD INTO HIM, PAST HIM - BOOMS UP AS IT APPROACHES SADIE. WHO STANDS AT FULL HEIGHT AS IT STOPS IN C.U.

TATE CONT.

8. LOW STICKS- JUST ABOVE GROUND - MED. FULL VOITYCK BY IRON FURNITURE - MED - TEX HOPS ON HIS LAP & WHACKS HIS HEAD 3 TIMES.

9. UP FROM GROUND. LOW - TEX WHOPS DUMMY HEAD - BUT REAL GOETZ HAND IN FGRD.

10. LOW ANGLE C.U. - TEX C.U. SNARL W/ EACH BLOW - BLOOD HITS HIM IN THE FACE.

11. LOW STICKS UP ONTO WINDOW - GUN & TEX'S HAND COME UP INTO FRAME SLINGIN BLOOD

12. HIGH STICKS - DOWN ONTO MED. OF TEX ON FRYKOWSKI, BASHING HIM 3 TIMES

13. LOW STICKS - C.U. - VOITYCK GETTING WHUMPED W/ GUN BUTT - 3 TIMES

TATE CONT.

14. HAND HELD - BEHIND THE BUNTLINE, 10mm CAM FOLLOWS THE BLOW DOWN & BACK FROM FRYKOWSKI'S HEAD

15. LOW STICKS - C.U. - SLO MO - GRIP BREAKS AS BUTT END SINKS INTO DUMMY GOO HEAD - GOETZ HAND OBSCURS DUMMY FACE IN FRED.

16. MED. 2 SHOT OF VOITYCK & TEX - TEX KNOCKS VOITYCK FLAT, CAM FLIPS 90° LEFT - FOLLOWING - HOLDS AS TEX STABS STABS

17. FROM ROOF - HIGH STICKS - OVERHEAD - TEX STABS STABS STABS STABS

18. LOW STICKS - MED. C.U. A HORRIFIED LINDA STEPS IN FR. RIGHT - ENTER FR. RIGHT

19. CAM STARTS LOW BEHIND LINDA REACTING - CAM CRANES UP & BACK DOLLIES REVEALING VOITYCK STANDING BEFORE

TATE CONT.

END POINT OF #19

20A. HIGH STICKS — SLIGHT ABOVE EYE LEVEL C.U. — LINDA'S FACE — "OH MY GOD, I'M SO SORRY!!"

20B. MED. C.U. HIGH STICKS — VOITYCK, DRIPPING BLOOD — "HELP ME..."

21. EYE LEVEL — (10mm?) CAM DOLLIES R TO L — WITH LINDA — & BOOM DOWN →

21. AS LINDA GOES TO THE DOOR — FROM WHICH SADIE EMERGES — THEY CONTINUE — STOPPING IN FRONT OF WINDOW — WHERE THE CAMERA ENDS IN A LOW ANGLE 2 SHOT — DIALOGUE

22. LOW ANGLE MED. C.U. — VOITYCK STAGGERING FOREWARD — CRYING FOR HELP — CAM DOLLIES BACKWARD IN FRONT OF HIM

FILMOGRAPHY

Catch Us If You Can (*aka* **Having A Wild Weekend**, John Boorman, 1965)
You're probably wondering what in the world this film is doing on the list. After all, it was made well before the murders. For that matter, Manson was still in jail when this film was released. In a nutshell, **CUIYC** is the story of a movie stuntman who runs off with England's top model. It was intended as a vehicle for the Dave Clark Five, who, at the time, were rivalling The Beatles in popularity. For that reason, this film is often compared to **Hard Day's Night**, but only by people who either never saw it, or didn't really watch it. While Richard Lester's Beatle film is lighthearted romp through England, **Catch Us If You Can** has a darker edge to it.

In one of the film's most disturbing scenes, Dave Clark and his "bird" stumble across a group of hippies that are living in the bombed-out remains of an Military Proving Ground. The group is led by a strangely mesmerizing figure who mouths Zen koans. Clearly the hippy leader was meant to resemble Jesus Christ, but historical hindsight has altered this image entirely.

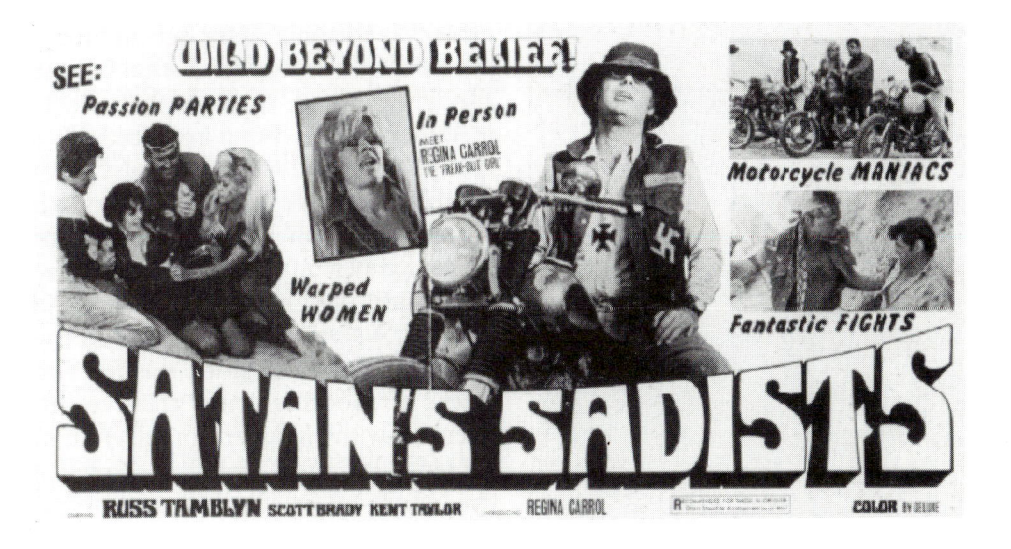

Satan's Sadists (Al Adamson, 1969)
Not really a Manson film at all, but that didn't stop Al Adamson from capitalizing on the case. Posters for this movie featured newspaper clips about the Manson family murders under the banner: "NOW: See on the screen the SHOCKING STORIES you are reading about in the

newspapers TODAY!" Also, Adamson filmed **The Female Bunch** (1969) on the Spahn Ranch, reputedly with members of the Family as extras.

Invocation Of My Demon Brother & Lucifer Rising (Kenneth Anger, 1969 & 1970)
Listed here for their connection to the Manson family through Manson's pal, Bobby Beausoleil. Beausoleil was found guilty and convicted of the 1969 slaying of Gary Hinman. Beausoleil wrote some of the music for **Lucifer Rising** (along with Jimmy Page), and starred in **Invocation Of My Demon Brother** (music for that one was by Mick Jagger). Beausoleil also appeared in the David Friedman produced sexploitation film, **The Ramrodders** (1969).

Gabrielle (Arlo Shiffen, 1970)
This cheesy little sexploitation film from Champaign, Illinois is completely forgotten today, but it does have the meaningless distinction of being the first Manson movie released – sort of. Gabrielle is the story of a young woman who, after a brutal rape, scars herself and winds up under the care of a psycho doctor named Matson. Dr. Matson is the head a group he calls the Family. The Family specializes in sexual excess and the occasional murder.

Gabrielle was released after Manson was captured, but the differences in the story suggest that some aspects of the film were tacked onto a film that was already in production when the news hit the streets. Naming the doctor Matson and calling his group the Family was most likely an afterthought, meant to take advantage of the hottest crime of the decade. Not that there's anything wrong with that; it is, after all, why it's called exploitation. (See also **Satan's Sadists**.)

Beyond The Valley Of The Dolls (Russ Meyer, 1970)
When Russ Meyer and Roger Ebert sat down to write the screenplay for this classic, they wanted to exploit as many topical issues as they could stuff into the film. According to Roger Ebert: "We knew we would have the murder orgy [in the film] (we were working before the Tate case was solved, and it was one of the exploitable elements we wanted to use)...." Ebert was working on the assumption that Tate, Folger, *et al* were in some way connected to their own deaths. One can only wonder what **BVD** would have turned out like if Ebert and Meyer had started working on the script a year later.

I Drink Your Blood (David Durston, 1970)
Clearly horror movies were the main benefactors when it came to the Manson family saga. Nowhere is this better demonstrated than Durston's **I Drink Your Blood**, the story of a murderously evil tribe of

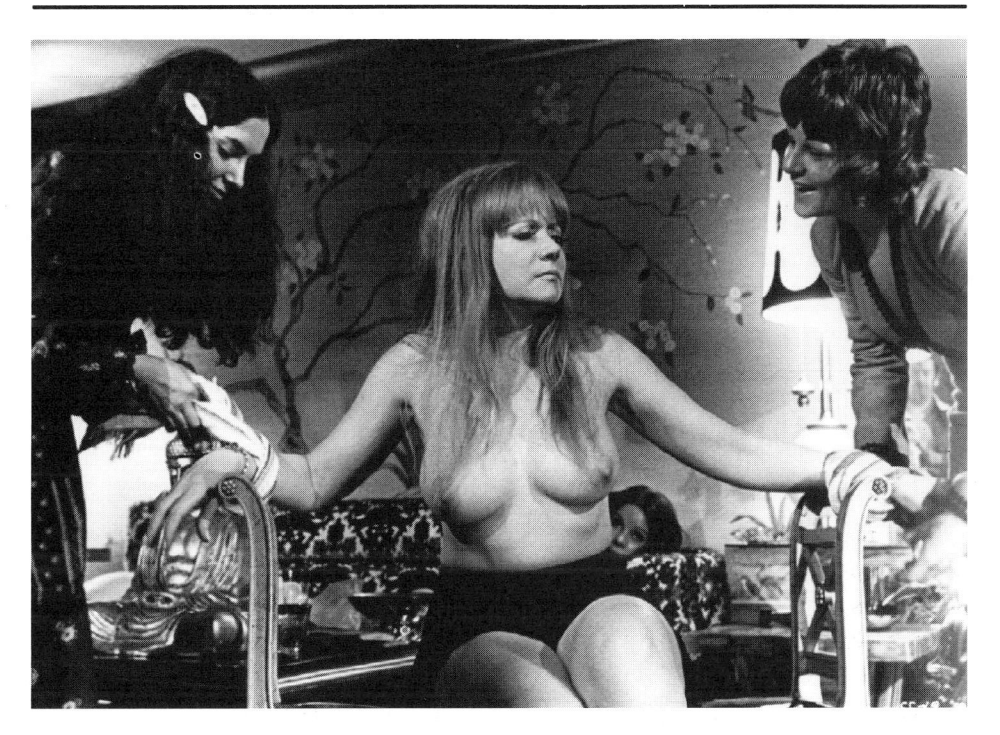

The Love Thrill Murders

hippies. After raping a woman and feeding an old man LSD, a young boy gets even with the group by feeding them rabies-infected meat pies. What follows is a fairly cheesy attack of the rabid hippies. The director apparently thought that hydrophobia was a literal feature of the disease. Good guys avoid attacks by the mad hipsters with help from the garden hose. This film is most famous for its release as part of a double bill: **I Eat Your Skin** and **I Drink Your Blood**. The former film is actually a 1964 black and white zombie movie (original title: **Voodoo Blood Bath**).

The Night God Screamed (Lee Madden, 1971)
This film was rarely seen until the age of VCRs gave it a whole new audience. Starring former Hollywood starlet Jeanne Crain, it is the story of a gang of Mansonesque Jesus Freaks that crucify a preacher and terrify his wife.

The Love Thrill Murders (*aka* **Sweet Savior**, Robert L. Roberts, 1971)
This film is a true oddity, and is the first fictionalized account of the Manson Murders put on film. The setting is switched to New York and the leader of the cult is a druggy character named Moon. Moon is played by former teen heart-throb, Troy Donahue. During the fifties, Troy Donahue was one of the hottest commodities in Hollywood. He

The Omega Man

starred in the hit TV shows *Surfside Six* and *Hawaii Eye* and appeared in dozens of major motion pictures, including Delmer Daves' **A Summer Place** and Joseph Strick's 1959 version of **Imitation Of Life**.

Along with Russ Tamblyn and Tab Hunter, Troy Donahue was one of the hottest young actors in Hollywood. Like Tamblyn and Hunter, when roles in Hollywood got scarce, Donahue went to low budget and alternative films for work. Donahue turns in a pretty good performance here as Moon, the leader of a hippy cult. Although all of the names have been changed, it's apparent that **Sweet Saviour** is the Manson story. Donahue went on from here to star in several low budget features, including **Blood Nasty, Assault Of The Party Nerds, Shock 'Em Dead**, and **Click: The Calendar Girl Killer**.

Omega Man (Boris Sagal, 1971)
1971 was a banner year for Manson movies. It was still too early to tell the story factually, but the case was very much on the minds of people everywhere. Exploitation and independent filmmakers were quick to capitalize on the case. Hollywood was a bit slower on the uptake; it was, after all, their story to begin with. One early attempt to put the Manson case in its proper perspective was **The Omega Man**. Based on the book *I Am Legend*, by Richard Matheson, **The Omega Man** follows Robert Neville (Charlton Heston) the lone survivor of a plague that kills nearly everyone in the world. The book had already been made into a movie a few years earlier (**The Last Man On Earth**, starring Vincent

Price). The earlier film was much closer to the original, but it becomes apparent that director Sagal has something else in mind. Heston spends much of his time reminiscing about the old days by watching **Woodstock**. Meanwhile an evil group calling itself "The Family" tries to rid itself (and the face of the Earth) of their arch-nemesis, Neville. Few people recognized it at the time, but **The Omega Man** is really about that crossroads in American history between the belief that Peace and Love could change the world, and the cold realization that there were forces at work that were darker and far more powerful than any utopian ideals.

Last House On The Left (Wes Craven, 1972)
Not really a Manson film *per se*. The family in this film was a real family, having more in common with Ma Barker. But there is no question that the events in California not only shaped this film, but gave its nastiness a believable edge. The film tells the story of two girls who are picked up hitchhiking by a family of psychos. After torturing the girls to death the psychos unknowingly make a stop at the parents of one of the girls. When the father figures out what has happened to his daughter, he and his wife take justice into their own hands – and mouth. If the story sounds vaguely familiar, it's because Ingmar Bergman used it in **The Virgin Spring**.

Deathmaster (Ray Danton, 1972)
An interesting variation on the Manson myth. Robert Quarry (of **Count Yorga** fame) plays Khorda, the leader of a hippy cult. This time, however, instead of turning out to be Manson, he turns out to be Dracula. Made on a shoestring budget, **Deathmaster** is a pretty cheesy, but fun to watch.

Manson (aka **The Other Side Of Madness**, Lawrence Merrick, 1972)
Rarely shown, this film features the Manson girls (most notably Squeaky Fromme and Sandra Good) in candid interviews before they wound up in prison themselves. For anyone interested in the Manson case, this one is required viewing for its inside information and its remarkably objective stance. Here we get to see – in its entirety – Manson's famous walk down the jail hallway. As photographers snapped his picture, Manson distorted his face in every way he could, from a beatific smile to an insane stare. Guess which face ended up on the cover of *Life* magazine. This scene, more than all the other scenes in all the other movies, explains both Charlie Manson and the public's impression of him.

Pink Flamingos (John Waters, 1972)
Not quite a Manson movie, but Waters does offer a tribute to his

176 • Charlie's Family

REVEALED FOR THE FIRST TIME
outside the courtroom
—the staggering details of the most
hideously bizarre murders in the
annals of crime

WE CANNOT DISCLOSE HOW SOME
OF THESE FILMS WERE OBTAINED
but you will hear the shocking
FACTS told in their own words
BY THE KILLERS THEMSELVES!

MANSON

A LAURENCE MERRICK FILM

ACADEMY AWARD NOMINEE
Best Feature-Length Documentary

COLOR by Movielab An AMERICAN INTERNATIONAL Release

favorite family with "Free Tex Watson" spray-painted on the side of a wall. Waters understood before anyone the potential shock appeal regarding the Manson family. Later on, Waters met Susan Atkins and Tex Watson and became friends with them. When it came to Manson, Waters expressed little interest in the man, saying that, since he didn't kill anyone, he didn't consider him in the same league with Watson and Atkins.

Texas Chainsaw Massacre (Tobe Hooper, 1974)
Although its roots are attributed to Ed Gein, there was always something distinctly Mansonesque about this film. It wasn't until a few years later, with the release of Wes Craven's **The Hills Have Eyes** that the connection became clear. As with **Last House On The Left** and **The Hills Have Eyes**, the family in **Texas Chainsaw Massacre** is a genetic family. Unlike the real Gein story, we have a trio of brothers here whose actions defy understanding. Had Hooper thrown in some sisters, the film's kinship to the Manson family would have been more obvious. Whether or not Tobe Hooper intended for this relationship is irrelevent. The Manson Family story has forever changed the meaning of the family (at least in horror movies).

Snuff (Roberta & Michael Findlay ["Allen Shackerton"], 1974)
What started as a forgettable attempt to film a fictional account of the Manson Family nearly ended up on the shelf. It eventually became one of the most notorious movies of the seventies, and is almost singlehandedly responsible for an urban myth that just won't go away.

Filming movies in America was getting expensive. Actors wanted too much money, which meant, simply, that they wanted to making a living wage for all their work. Shooting with sound also raised the costs of filmmaking considerably. Sleaze director Michael Findlay thought he'd figured out the perfect solution to this problem. He went down to Argentina and filmed a movie called **The Slaughter**. He used a local cast that asked for far less remuneration than their New York counterparts. Also, since the movie was going to be dubbed into English anyway, he didn't even bother with sound set-ups, choosing, instead, to shoot the entire film MOS (without sound).

When the movie was finished, it was too crummy even for the exploitation distributors (this seems hard to believe). The movie seemed destined for the dustbin until Allen Shackerton had the brilliant idea of tacking some meaningless gore footage onto the very end of the film. The claim was that this was actual footage of a murder caught on film and smuggled into the country on the end of the Findlay film. The rumored existence of a "snuff" film was making the rounds at the time, so the movie became a must see for the morbid and the curious. Most amazing of all was that some people actually believed that the patently fake footage at the end of the film was real.

Helter Skelter (Tom Gries, 1976)
This Made-for-TV movie is based on Prosecutor Vincent Bugliosi's outrageously self-aggrandizing book of the same name. It isn't a great

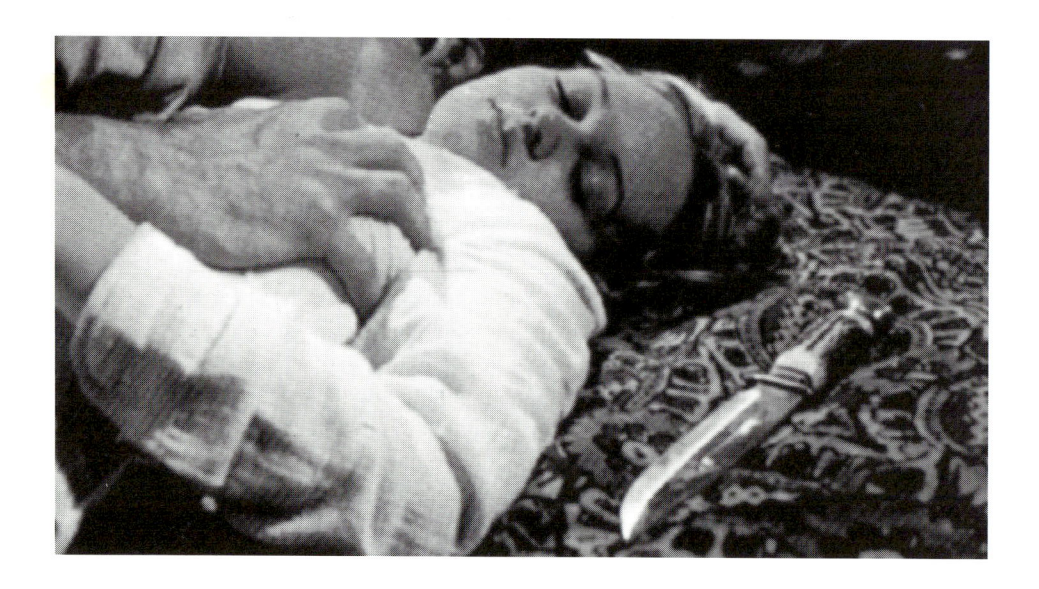

Snuff

Helter Skelter

film, but it *is* better than the book. At least we don't have to listen to Bugliosi crow like a banty cock about his legal prowess.

While watching it, I couldn't help but wonder what Jack Webb would have done with this screenplay. By the end, I found myself wishing Jack Webb *had* directed it. Tom Gries clearly confuses emoting with emotion here. Steven Railsback (of **The Stunt Man**) turns in an entertaining, over-the-top performance, threatening to chew his way right out of the television set. Marilyn Burns (of **Texas Chainsaw Massacre** fame) is well cast, but no less hysterical, as Linda Kasabian.

In spite of its hokey histrionics, **Helter Skelter** is worth watching. It covers the important legal aspects of the case with a thoroughness that only someone on the inside could have provided. Like the book, it makes the L.A. police out to be the most inept law enforcement organization since the Keystone Kops – a reputation they've worked hard to earn. It is also a prime example of the seventies-style made-for-TV movie with countless zoom shots and bad lighting.

The Hills Have Eyes (Wes Craven, 1977)
Wes Craven returned to the Manson Family for inspiration in his second feature. Taking equal parts of the Sawney Beane story (a Scottish cannibal family), and the Manson Family history (Charlie and the Family liked to go to Death Valley and eventually planned to live there), Wes Craven created a film that, like his previous effort, shocked many viewers. Thanks to some heavy doses of humor, however, this film is considerably easier for most people to sit through (although no one has ever taken such a poll, **Last House On The Left** surely ranks as one of the most walked-out-of movies of all time).

Manson Family Movies (John Aes-Nihil, 1984)
An interesting attempt to recreate home movies as they might have been made by the Manson family. I must admit, the whole thing seemed fake to me, but some of the people I watched it with thought it was real, so I guess John Aes-Nihil succeeded where other have failed. The movie does capture a certain level a creepiness that Pettibon's **Judgment Day Theatre** (1989) lacks.

Stryker's War (*aka* **Thou Shalt Not Kill, Except...**, Josh Becker, 1985)
A man returns home from Viet Nam, hoping to leave the war behind him, but an evil cult leader (played by director, Sam Raimi) forces him into a showdown. Set in 1969, there are references to Manson and other events of the time.

Death Valley '69 (Richard Kern & Judith Barry, 1986)
Splatterpunk Richard Kern does his take on Manson in the form of a

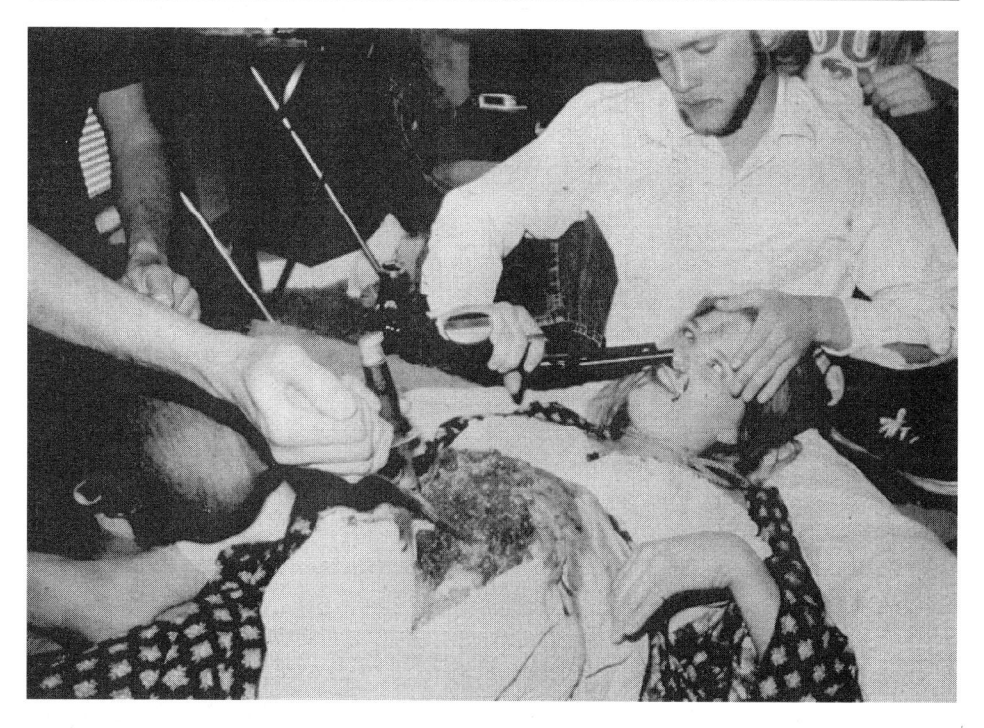

Manson Family Movies

rock video featuring Sonic Youth. The Manson story is merged with modern punk imagery showing the continuum between Manson's anti-hippies and punks.

8-8-88 (1988)
On August 8, 1988, Boyd Rice (Non), Anton's estranged daughter Zeena LaVey, Radio Werewolf leader Nikolas Schreck, American Front leader Bob Heick and Feral House publisher Adam Parfrey got together, ostensibly to celebrate the Tate-LaBianca murders of twenty years earlier, but mostly to try and shock the hipsters in San Francisco. The results were mixed, to be kind. Also shown that night was **The Other Side of Madness** (see **Manson**). The video box suggests that the film might also be on this tape, but it is not. The tape is merely home videorecorder account of the evening, followed by some tepid interviews by the major players.

Charles Manson, Superstar (Nikolas Schreck, 1989)
A revisionist documentary by Southern Californian Nicolas Schreck, author of *The Manson Files*. Schreck intersperses segments from an interview he conducted with Manson back in the late eighties with hyperbolic statements about Manson's relative innocence. Manson – as we have learned from watching too many interviews – always tells an

Death Valley 69

interviewer exactly what he or she wants to hear, and this one is no exception. Schreck's schtick at the time was Satanism, so we get Charlie the Satanist. Schreck's biographical notes are delivered in a sleep-inducing monotone, which is too bad because Schreck is capable of a forceful delivery when he feels like it. Maybe his heart just wasn't in it.

Judgment Day Theatre: The Book Of Manson (Raymond Pettibon, 1989)
There is an important clue as to what to expect from this film in its title: **Judgement Day *Theatre***. This thing sounds too much like a third-rate theatre piece to be anything else. Considering how badly *good* plays translates to the screen, you can imagine the results with this piece of dreck. Think of a John Waters film without humor that thinks it's clever and you'll get some idea of what's in store for you if you rent this thing. Pettibon postulates on possible meetings between Jimi Hendrix, Norman Mailer and a pre-Tate murder Roman Polanski. The whole thing appears to have been filmed at a suburban tract home somewhere in the mid-West. Ultra-skippable.

Manson '92 (1992)
This bootleg video is a tape of Manson's 1992 parole hearing as it appeared on Court TV. Compare this interview (for that is what it

Charles Manson, Superstar (© Joe Coleman)

essentially is) with the one Nikolas Schreck had conducted a few years earlier for a good example of Manson changing his tune to please the listener. After this hearing, Manson was denied any parole hearings for five years. Hopefully Parole official Ron Koenig spent that time learning how to pronounce Terre Haute and Bobby Beausoleil. Manson's usual interview tricks (sophistry, asking questions to avoid answering them, etc.) just won't fly here and he seems to know it. By the end of the hearing he is fighting back the tears as he realizes he has to spend at least five more years in jail.

Manson And Me (Matthew Mahan, 1997)
This is not a movie, but a theatre piece written by Richard Rubacher, a former psychiatric worker for the California Department of Social Services.

The Butcher Boy (Neil Jordan, 1998)
Not a Manson movie at all but a good example of the extent to which the Manson mythology pervades our psyches. When the mean little protagonist Francy breaks into the house of his arch-enemy, Mrs. T, and scrawls "Pig" on all the walls, we can't help but think about the Manson Family's similar behaviour at the Tate-Polanski house.

—**Jim Morton**

DEATH TRIP

THE STORY OF CHARLES MANSON AND THE LOVE AND TERROR CULT

BIBLIOGRAPHY

Atkins, Susan, with Slosser, Bob; *Child Of Satan, Child Of God*; Logos International; Plainfied, New Jersey; 1977; ISBN 0-88270-276-9

Baer, Rosemary; *Reflections On The Manson Trial*; Word Books; Waco, Texas; 1972

Bishop, George; *Witness To Evil*; Nash Publishing; Los Angeles; 1971

Bravin, Jess; *Squeaky – The Life And Times Of Lynette Alice Fromme*; St. Martin's Press; New York; 1997; ISBN 0-312-15663-4

Bugliosi, Vincent T., and Gentry, Curt; *Helter Skelter*; W. W. Norton & Company, Incorporated; New York, 1994

Cooper, David E.; *The Manson Murders: A Philosophical Inquiry*; Schenkman Books, Inc.; Rochester, Vermont; 1974; ISBN 0-87073-533-0

Emmons, Nuel; *Manson In His Own Words*; Grove Press Inc.; New York; 1986; ISBN 0-394-55558-9

Endleman, Robert; *Jonestown And The Manson Family*; Psyche Press, New York; 1993; ISBN 0-9622885-5-1

Gilmore, John, and Kenner, Ron; *The Garbage People*; Omega Press; Los Angeles; 1971

Harrington, William G.; *The Helter Skelter Murders* (Columbo), Vol. 1; Forge; May 1995

Leblanc, Jerry, and Davis, Ivor; *Five To Die*; Holloway House Publishing Co.; Los Angeles; 1970; ISBN 87067-306-8

Livsey, Clara; *The Manson Women*; Richard Marek Publishers; New York; 1980; ISBN 0-399-90073-X

Murphy, Bob; *Desert Shadows*; Falcon Press; Billings, Montana; 1986; ISBN 0-934318-86-7

Nelson, Bill; *Tex Watson, The Man, The Madness, The Manipulation*; Pen Power Publications; 1991; ISBN 0-9629084-0-1

Nelson, Bill; *Manson Behind The Scenes*; Pen Power Publications; 1997; ISBN 0-9629084-1-X

Russell, J.D.; *Charles Manson, A Chronicle Of Death*; Apollo Books; Woodbridge, Connecticut; 1971; ISBN 524-00125-100

Sanders, Ed; *The Family*; E. P. Dutton & Co. Inc.; New York; 1971; ISBN 77-125906

Satan, Johnny; *Death Trip: The Story Of Charles Manson & The Love And Terror Cult*; Death Valley Books; Arlington, 1994; DV 001

Schiller, Lawrence; *The Killing Of Sharon Tate*; The New American Library, Inc.; New York; 1970

Schreck, Nikolas; *The Manson File*; Amok Press; New York; 1988

Terry, Maury; *The Ultimate Evil*; Doubleday & Co., Inc.; New York;1987; ISBN 0-385-23452-X

Watkins, Paul, with Soledad, Guillermo; *My Life With Charles Manson*; Bantam Books; New York; 1979; ISBN 0-553-12788-8

Watson, Charles, and Chaplain Ray; *Will You Die For Me?*; Cross Roads Publications, Inc.; Dallas, Texas; ISBN 0-8007-0912-8

Wizinski, Sy; *Charles Manson, Love Letters To A Secret Disciple*; Moonmad Press; Terre Haute, Indiana; 1976; ISBN 0-917918-01-0

Zaehner, R. C.; *Our Savage God*; Universal Press Syndicate; New York; 1974; ISBN 0-8362-0611-8

Zamora, William; *Trial By Your Peers (Blood Family)*; Zebra Books; Kensington Publishing Co.; New York; 1973

INDEX OF FILMS

Page number in bold indicates an illustration

A
ASSAULT OF THE PARTY NERDS — 174

B
BEYOND THE VALLEY OF THE DOLLS — 172
BLOOD NASTY — 174
BUTCHER BOY — 183

C
CATCH US IF YOU CAN — 171
CHARLES MANSON, SUPERSTAR — 167, 180–181, **182**
CHARLIE'S FAMILY — 5, 6, 8, 9–163, **14**, **15**, **18**, **19**, **22**, **24**, **25**, **27**, **29**, **31**, **36**, **39**, **40**, **41**, **45**, **46**, **48**, **50**, **51**, **52**, **55**, **63**, **70**, **71**, **73**, **75**, **76**, **77**, **78**, **79**, **80**, **83**, **86**, **88**, **91**, **92**, **93**, **98**, **100**, **103**, **104**, **106**, **107**, **111**, **112**, **114**, **117**, **118**, **121**, **123**, **124**, **125**, **127**, **128**, **131**, **132**, **133**, **134**, **135**, **141**, **143**, **144**, **146**, **147**, **149**, 151–163, **164**, 165
CHUNKBLOWER — 7
CLICK: THE CALENDER GIRL KILLER — 174
COUNT YORGA — 175

D
DAWN OF THE DEAD — 7
DEADBEAT AT DAWN — 6, 7
DEATH VALLEY 69 — 179–180, **181**
DEATHMASTER, THE — 175
DRACULA — 167

E
8-8-88 — 180

F
FEMALE BUNCH, THE — 172
FLESH TRILOGY — 165

G
GABRIELLE — 172
GLORY STOMPERS, THE — 6

H
HARD DAY'S NIGHT — 171
HELL'S ANGELS '69 — 6
HELL'S ANGELS ON WHEELS — 6
HELTER SKELTER — 167, 177–179, **178**
HILLS HAVE EYES, THE — 177, 179

I
I DRINK YOUR BLOOD — 172–173
I EAT YOUR SKIN — 173

J
JUDGMENT DAY THEATRE — 179, 181

K

L
LAST HOUSE ON THE LEFT — 167, 175, 177, 179
LAST MAN ON EARTH, THE — 175
LOVE THRILL MURDERS, THE — **173**, 173–174
LUCIFER RISING — 172

M
MANSON	5, 175, **176**, 180
MANSON '92	182–183
MANSON FAMILY MOVIES	179, **180**
MY SWEET SATAN	7, **8**

N
NIGHT GOD SCREAMED, THE	173

O
OLGA	165
OMEGA MAN, THE	**174**, 174–175

P
PINK FLAMINGOS	175–177

Q

R
RAMRODDERS, THE	172

S
SATAN'S SADISTS	**171**, 171–172
SEEING RED	6
SHOCK 'EM DEAD	174
SNUFF	177, **178**
STRYKER'S WAR	179
STUNT MAN, THE	179
SUMMER PLACE, A	174

T
TEXAS CHAINSAW MASSACRE, THE	167, 177, 179

U

V
VIRGIN SPRING, THE	175

W
WILD ANGELS	6
WOODSTOCK	175

X

Y
YOU KILLED ME FIRST	62, 64, **65**

Z

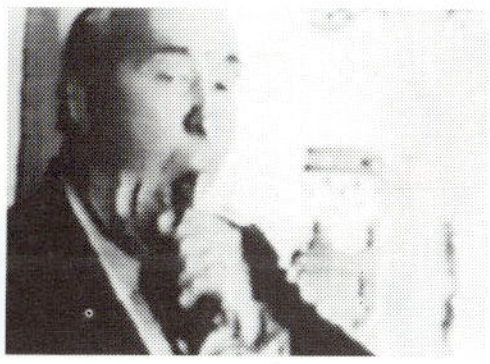

CREATION CINEMA COLLECTION

1. KILLING FOR CULTURE
Kerekes & Slater

Killing For Culture is a definitive investigation into the urban myth of the "snuff movie". Includes: FEATURE FILM – from *Peeping Tom* to *Videodrome* and beyond; MONDO FILM – from *Mondo Cane* to present day 'shockumentaries'; DEATH FILM – from *Faces Of Death* to real deaths captured on film such as live-TV suicides, executions, and news footage.

Illustrated by stunning photographs from cinema, documentary and real life, **Killing For Culture** is a necessary book which examines and questions the human obsession with images of violence, dismemberment and death, and the way our society is coping with an increased profusion of these disturbing yet compelling images from all quarters. Includes filmography and index.

"Well-researched and highly readable, Killing For Culture *is a must-have*."
– FILM THREAT

CINEMA/CULTURE   Trade Paperback   1 871592 20 8   169 x 244mm   288 pages   £14.95

2. INSIDE TERADOME
Jack Hunter

Freakshows – human anomalies presented for spectacle – have flourished throughout recorded history. The birth of the movies provided a further outlet for these displays, which in turn led to a peculiar strain of bizarre cinema: Freak Film. **Inside Teradome** is a comprehensive, fully illustrated guide to the roots and development of this fascinating, often disturbing cinematic genre.

Including: Teratology: freaks in myth and medicine; the history of freakshows, origins of cinema; influence of sideshows on cinema; use of human anomalies in cinema; freaks and geeks; bizarre cinema: mutilation and other fetishes; illustrated filmography; index; over 350 photographs. From the real-life grotesqueries of Tod Browning's *Freaks*, to the modern nightmare vision of *Santa Sangre*, **Inside Teradome** reveals a twisted thread of voyeuristic sickness running both through cinema and the society it mirrors.

CINEMA/CULTURE   Trade Paperback   1 871592 41 0   169 x 244mm   256 pages   £14.95

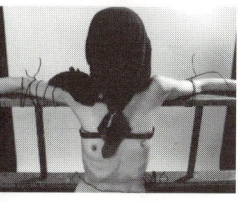

3. DEATHTRIPPING
Jack Sargeant

Deathtripping is an illustrated history, account and critique of the "Cinema Of Transgression", providing a long-overdue and comprehensive documentation of this essential modern sub-cultural movement. Including: A brief history of underground/trash cinema: seminal influences including Andy Warhol, Jack Smith, George and Mike Kuchar, John Waters. Interviews with key film-makers, including Richard Kern, Nick Zedd, Cassandra Stark, Beth B, Tommy Turner; plus associates such as Joe Coleman, Lydia Lunch, Lung Leg and David Wojnarowicz. Notes and essays on transgressive cinema, philosophy of transgression; manifestos, screen-plays; film index and bibliography.

Heavily illustrated with rare and sometimes disturbing photographs, **Deathtripping** is a unique guide to a style of film-making whose impact and influence can no longer be ignored.

CINEMA/CULTURE   Trade Paperback   1 871592 29 1   169 x 244mm   256 pages   £11.95

4. FRAGMENTS OF FEAR
Andy Boot

Fragments Of Fear is an illustrated history of an often neglected film genre: the British Horror Movie. The book examines a wide range of British horror films, and the stories behind them, from the early melodramas of Tod Slaughter right through to Hammer and their rivals Tigon and Amicus, plus mavericks like Michael Reeves, sex/horror director Peter Walker and more recent talents such as Clive Barker, director of *Hellraiser*. Films discussed range in scope from the sadism of *Peeping Tom* to the mutant SF of *A Clockwork Orange* and the softcore porn/horror of Jose Larraz' *Vampyres*.

With plentiful illustrations, author Andy Boot unravels a tangled history and discovers many little-known gems amid the more familiar images of Hammer, including a wealth of exploitational cinema, to establish the British horror movie as a genre which can easily stand up to its more lauded American counterpart in the depth and diversity of its scope.

CINEMA   Trade Paperback   1 871592 35 6   169 x 244mm   288 pages   £12.95

CREATION BOOKS

CREATION CINEMA COLLECTION

5. DESPERATE VISIONS
Jack Stevenson

John Waters is the notorious director of *Pink Flamingos, Female Trouble, Desperate Living* and *Hairspray*, amongst other cult movie classics.

Desperate Visions features several in-depth interviews with Waters, as well as with members of his legendary entourage including Divine, Mary Vivian Pearce, Mink Stole and Miss Jean Hill. George & Mike Kuchar are the directors of such low-budget/underground classics as *Sins Of The Fleshapoids* and *Hold Me While I'm Naked*. Their visionary trash aesthetic was a great influence on the young John Waters.

Desperate Visions includes extensive interviews with the Kuchars, as well as a comprehensive assessment of their career and influence. Also included is a unique feature on actress Marion Eaton, star of the gothic porn epic *Thundercrack!*.

With many rare photographs, filmography and index, *Desperate Visions* is an essential introduction to the wild world of John Waters, and to the outrageous camp/underground film tradition which his movies exemplify.

CINEMA/CULTURE   Trade Paperback   1 871592 34 8   169 x 244mm   256 pages   £14.95

6. THE NAKED LENS
Jack Sargeant

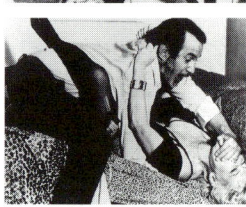

The Naked Lens is a vital collection of essays and interviews focusing on the most significant interfaces between the Beat writers, Beat culture and cinema; films by, featuring, or inspired by: WILLIAM S BURROUGHS • ALLEN GINSBERG • JACK KEROUAC • CHARLES BUKOWSKI • BRION GYSIN ANTHONY BALCH • RON RICE JOHN CASSAVETES • ANDY WARHOL • BOB DYLAN • KLAUS MAECK • GUS VAN SANT & many others

Including interviews with writers such as Allen Ginsberg, directors such as Robert Frank and actors such as Taylor Mead; plus detailed examination of key Beat texts and cult classics such as *Pull My Daisy, Chappaqua, Towers Open Fire* and *The Flower Thief*; verité and performance films such as *Shadows, Don't Look Back* and *Wholly Communion*; B-movies such as *The Subterraneans, Beat Generation* and Roger Corman's *Bucket Of Blood*; and Hollywood-style adaptations from *Heart Beat* and *Barfly* through to Cronenberg's *Naked Lunch*.

CINEMA/BEAT CULTURE   Trade Paperback   1 871592 67 4   169 x 244mm   288 pages   £12.95

7. HOUSE OF HORROR
Jack Hunter

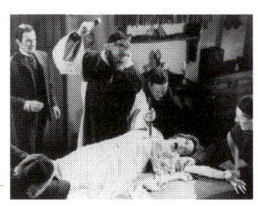

HAMMER FILMS remains one of the most successful and legendary of all British film companies. Their name is synonymous with gothic horror throughout the world.

House Of Horror traces the complete history of Hammer, from its early origins through to its golden era of classic horror movies, and presents a comprehensive overview of Hammer's importance and influence in world cinema.

House Of Horror includes interviews with Hammer stars Christopher Lee and Peter Cushing, detailed analysis of all Hammer's horror and fantasy films and their key directors, and dozens of rare and exciting photographs and posters; plus a fully illustrated A–Z of key Hammer personnel from both sides of the camera, a directory of unfilmed projects, a complete filmography, and full film index. **Third, expanded edition**

CINEMA   Trade Paperback   1 871592 19 4   169 x 244mm   224 pages   £12.95

8. MEAT IS MURDER!
Mikita Brottman

Violent death, murder, mutilation, eating and defaecation, ritualism, bodily extremes; cannibalism combines these crucial themes to represent one of the most symbolically charged narratives in the human psychic repertoire.

As a grotesque figure of power, threat, and atavistic appetites, the cannibal has played a formidable role in the tales told by members of all cultures – whether oral, written, or filmic – and embodies the ultimate extent of transgressive behaviour to which human beings can be driven.

Meat Is Murder! is a unique and explicit exploration of the stories that are told about cannibals, from classical myth to contemporary film and fiction, and features an in-depth illustrated critique of cannibalism as portrayed in the cinema, from mondo and exploitation films to horror movies and arthouse classics. It also details the atrocious crimes of real life cannibals of the modern age, such as Albert Fish, Ed Gein, Jeffrey Dahmer and Andrei Chikatilo.

CINEMA/CULTURE   Trade Paperback   1 871592 90 9   169 x 244mm   208 pages   £14.95

CREATION CINEMA COLLECTION

9 EROS IN HELL
Jack Hunter

SEX: The history of "pink" movies, from *Daydream* to *Ai No Corrida* and beyond, including the pop avant-garde violence of Koji Wakamatsu films such as *Violated Angels* and *Violent Virgin*. Bondage and S/M from *Moju* to *Captured For Sex* and Kinbiken rope torture.

BLOOD: From *Shogun Assassin* and *Psycho Junkie* to the killing orgies of *Guinea Pig* and *Atrocity*; from the "pink horror" nightmare *Entrails Of A Virgin* to the post-punk yakuza bloodbaths of Kei Fujiwara's *Organ* and Takashi Miike's *Fudoh*.

MADNESS: Homicidal psychosis, hallucination, mutation: *Tetsuo, Death Powder*, the films of Shozin Fukui such as *Pinocchio 964* and *Rubber's Lover*. Post-punk excess, nihilism, violence, suicide: *Labyrinth Of Dreams, Squareworld, Tokyo Crash*.

Eros In Hell examines all these movies and many more besides, is profusely illustrated with rare and unusual photographs, comprising a unique guide to the most prolific, fascinating and controversial underground/alternative cinema in the world.

CINEMA   Trade paperback   1 871592 93 3   169 x 244 mm   256 pages   £14.95

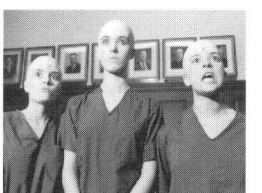

10 CHARLIE'S FAMILY
Jim VanBebber

Charles Manson and The Family. The Love and Terror Cult. The Dune Buggy Attack Battalion. Devil's Witches, Devil's Hole. Jim Van Bebber's mind-blowing movie **Charlie's Family** is the most accurate and uncompromising cinematic portrayal of the exterminating angels of Death Valley '69, a psychotic assault of sex, drugs and violence that propels the viewer headlong into the Manson experience.

Charlie's Family reconstructs the cataclysms of creepy-crawl and the Tate/La Bianca murders in vivid relief, showing us not only a devastating acid blood orgy but also the ways in which one man's messianic power held sway over an entire killer korps of sexually submissive yet homicidal believers.

The illustrated screenplay of **Charlie's Family** contains nearly 100 amazing photographs, including 16 in full colour, as well as the complete script and 16 original storyboards. It also includes the definitive illustrated essay on Manson-related movies, written by Jim Morton, main contributor to *Incredibly Strange Films*, as well as an introduction by esteemed underground film critic Jack Sargeant.

CINEMA/TRUE CRIME   Trade paperback   1 871592 94 1   169 x 244 mm   192 pages   £14.95

11 RENEGADE SISTERS
Bev Zalcock

From boarding school to women's prison, biker packs to urban vigilantes, rampaging girl gangs have long been a staple feature of exploitation/independent cinema.

Renegade Sisters examines the whole history of girl gangs on film, focusing on B-classics like Russ Meyer's *Faster, Pussycat! Kill! Kill!*, Herschell Gordon Lewis' *She-Devils On Wheels*, and Jack Hill's *Switchblade Sisters*; Women-In-Prison movies such as Stephanie Rothman's *Terminal Island* and Jack Hill's *Big Doll House*, with Pam Grier; camp SF like *Cat Women Of The Moon* and *Queen Of Outer Space*; plus many other deviant displays of girl power from various genres, right through to Todd Morris and Deborah Twiss' ferocious, post-Tarantino *A Gun For Jennifer*.

Renegade Sisters also looks at Queercore girls; the feminist/lesbian movies of Barbara Hammer, Jennifer Reeder, Anie Stanley and others, and includes interviews with film makers Vivienne Dick and Julie Jenkins, as well as *A Gun For Jennifer* writer/producer Deborah Twiss. With dozens of photographic illustrations.

CINEMA/WOMEN'S STUDIES   Trade paperback   1 871592 92 5   169 x 244 mm   208 pages   £14.95

CREATION BOOKS

ALSO AVAILABLE

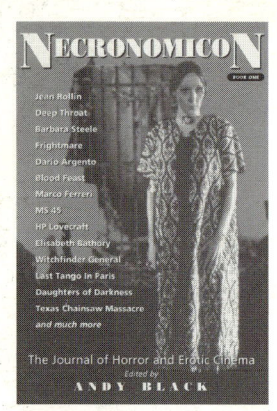

NECRONOMICON 1 — *Andy Black (ed)*

Necronomicon Book One continues the singular, thought-provoking exploration of transgressive cinema begun by the much-respected and acclaimed magazine of the same name. The transition to annual book format has allowed for even greater depth and diversity within the journal's trademarks of progressive critique and striking photographic content.

Including: MARCO FERRERI • TEXAS CHAINSAW MASSACRE • BARBARA STEELE • FRIGHTMARE • JEAN ROLLIN • DEEP THROAT • DARIO ARGENTO • LAST TANGO IN PARIS • H P LOVECRAFT • WITCHFINDER GENERAL • HERSCHELL GORDON LEWIS • EVIL DEAD • ABEL FERRARA *and much more*

CINEMA   Trade Paperback   1 871592 37 2   169 x 244mm   192 pages   £11.95

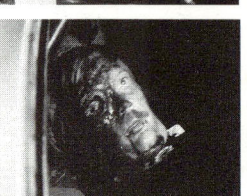

NECRONOMICON 2 — *Andy Black (ed)*

Book Two of the journal of horror and erotic cinema, continuing the thought-provoking exploration of transgressive film making begun by the first volume. With more illustrated insights into the world of celluloid sex and violence, including:

JESUS FRANCO • SADEAN CINEMA • RUSS MEYER • MANSON, POLANSKI, MACBETH • NEW JAPANESE PORNO • GEORGE A ROMERO • SS EXPLOITATION • BABA YAGA/CEMETERY MAN • WALERIAN BOROWCZYK • DARIO ARGENTO • FEMALE VAMPIRES • SE7EN *and much more*

"Lovingly produced and amply illustrated... engaging... Heady stuff."
—Sight & Sound

CINEMA   Trade paperback   1 871592 38 2   169 x 244mm   192 pages   £12.95

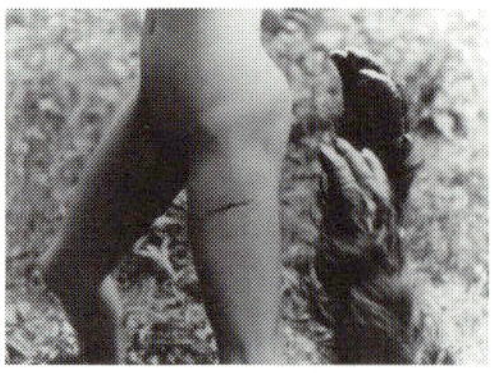

MAIL ORDER FORM   *(please photocopy if you do not wish to cut up your book)*

TITLE (please tick box)	PRICE(UK)	PRICE(US)	QTY
☐ Killing for Culture	£14.95	$19.95	
☐ Inside Teradome	£14.95	$19.95	
☐ Deathtripping	£11.95	$16.95	
☐ Fragments of Fear	£12.95	$17.95	
☐ Desperate Visions	£14.95	$19.95	
☐ The Naked Lens	£12.95	$19.95	
☐ House of Horror	£12.95	$19.95	
☐ Meat Is Murder!	£14.95	$19.95	
☐ Eros In Hell	£14.95	$19.95	
☐ Charlie's Family	£14.95	$19.95	
☐ Renegade Sisters	£14.95	$19.95	
☐ Necronomicon 1	£11.95	$16.95	
☐ Necronomicon 2	£12.95	$17.95	

☐ I enclose cheque/money order/cash

☐ I wish to pay by   ☐ Visa   ☐ Mastercard

Card No: |_|_|_|_| |_|_|_|_| |_|_|_|_| |_|_|_|_|

Expiry Date _____

Signature _____   Date _____

Name_____

Address_____

_____

_____

SUBTOTAL _____

P&P _____

TOTAL _____

UK: Add 10% to total price for p&p. EUROPE: Add 15%. Payment with order to: Creation Books, 83 Clerkenwell Road. London EC1R 5AR (£sterling only).
US: Add 10% to total price for p&p. REST OF THE WORLD: Add 20%. Payment with order to: Creation Books, PO Box 13512, Berkeley, CA 94712 (US$ only)

CREATION BOOKS